Schleiermacher

BLOOMSBURY GUIDES FOR THE PERPLEXED

Bloomsbury's Guides for the Perplexed are clear, concise and accessible introductions to thinkers, writers and subjects that students and readers can find especially challenging. Concentrating specifically on what it is that makes the subject difficult to grasp, these books explain and explore key themes and ideas, guiding the reader towards a thorough understanding of demanding material.

Guides for the Perplexed available from Bloomsbury include:

Balthasar: A Guide for the Perplexed, Rodney Howsare
Benedict XVI: A Guide for the Perplexed, Tracey Rowland
Bonhoeffer: A Guide for the Perplexed, Joel Lawrence
Calvin: A Guide for the Perplexed, Paul Helm
De Lubac: A Guide for the Perplexed, David Grumett
Luther: A Guide for the Perplexed, David M. Whitford
Pannenberg: A Guide for the Perplexed, Timothy Bradshaw
Tillich: A Guide for the Perplexed, Andrew O'Neil
Wesley: A Guide for the Perplexed, Jason A. Vickers
Žižek: A Guide for the Perplexed, Sean Sheehan

A GUIDE FOR THE PERPLEXED

Schleiermacher

THEODORE VIAL

BLOOMSBURY
LONDON • NEW DELHI • NEW YORK • SYDNEY

Bloomsbury T&T Clark
An imprint of Bloomsbury Publishing Plc

50 Bedford Square
London
WC1B 3DP
UK

1385 Broadway
New York
NY 10018
USA

www.bloomsbury.com

Bloomsbury is a registered trade mark of Bloomsbury Publishing Plc

First published 2013

© Theodore Vial, 2013

All rights reserved. No part of this publication may be reproduced or transmitted in any form or by any means, electronic or mechanical, including photocopying, recording, or any information storage or retrieval system, without prior permission in writing from the publishers.

Theodore Vial has asserted his right under the Copyright, Designs and Patents Act, 1988, to be identified as Author of this work.

No responsibility for loss caused to any individual or organization acting on or refraining from action as a result of the material in this publication can be accepted by Bloomsbury Academic or the author.

British Library Cataloguing-in-Publication Data
A catalogue record for this books is available from the British Library.

ISBN: HB: 978-0-567-52009-8
PB: 978-0-567-41598-1

Library of Congress Cataloging-in-Publication Data
Vial, Theodore
Schleiermacher: A Guide for the Perplexed/Theodore Vial
p.cm
Includes bibliographic references and index.
ISBN 978-0-567-52009-8 (hardcover) – ISBN 978-0-567-41598-1 (pbk.)
2012045678

Typeset by Newgen Imaging Systems Pvt Ltd, Chennai, India

For Alice and Ted Vial,
who know a good preacher when they see one

CONTENTS

Acknowledgments viii

Introduction 1
1   Life and Times   4
2   Schleiermacher's Worldview   24
3   Hermeneutics   47
4   On Religion   60
5   Mediating Theology   82
6   Schleiermacher as Political Activist   101
Conclusion   118

Notes   120
Select Bibliography   141
Index   149

ACKNOWLEDGMENTS

It has been a bit too long since I have published a book, and so the intellectual and personal debts accrued are many. My appreciation for the nineteenth century was born in Wendell Dietrich's classroom at Brown University, and cultivated by my dissertation director, Brian Gerrish, at The University of Chicago. Anyone familiar with those two scholars will know that they set an intimidatingly high bar, which I never claim to clear but to which I always aspire.

At Chicago Brian (Mr Gerrish, at the time) formed an *Arbeitskreis* that met regularly to undertake common projects and to critique each other's work. One of the unexpected benefits of being a Gerrish student is that this *Arbeitskreis* has continued to meet and to function well beyond the time and place of our graduate studies. Jim Brandt, Paul Capetz, Dawn DeVries, Julia Lamm, Brent Sockness, Walt Wyman, and for a long time now Dick Crouter, as an honorary member, have continued to get together to talk shop, and have proved willing to drop other responsibilities to read and give feedback over the years. Walt Wyman gave insightful and kind feedback on Chapter 4 of this book. The continuing work and friendship of this group is evidence for me in support of Schleiermacher's claims about the ways groups form around and embody the personality of their founders.

Andrew Dole has been a valued conversation partner over the years. He is the one who gave my name to T&T Clark. His own efforts toward a better reading of Schleiermacher's theory of religion has been very important for my own work. He read and commented on Chapters 2 and 4.

The Iliff School of Theology has provided an environment very conducive to thinking and writing. I am grateful to my colleagues on the faculty at Iliff and at the University of Denver, with whom we share a joint Ph.D. program, for feedback and for conversations that push my thinking. Special thanks to Dean Albert Hernández for providing a good scholarly environment in ways tangible and intangible. Two of the most important tangible ways have been protecting faculty research time, and protecting faculty from flying administrative shrapnel. I am particularly fortunate to have landed at a place that is the institutional home of two quite prominent Schleiermacher scholars, Cathie Kelsey and Terry Tice. Both read and commented on Chapter 1. To have had the chance to work with Richard Crouter, B. A. Gerrish, and Terrence Tice, the Holy Trinity of the generation of English-speaking Schleiermacher scholars preceding mine, is a gift given to few.

One of the great privileges of being at Iliff is the opportunity to work with a remarkable set of graduate students, both masters and Ph.D. Mary Ragan, Ben Sanders, and Sarah Scherer read the entire manuscript during their summer, and gave me invaluable feedback. Dave Scott did the same for Chapter 2. These students may be approaching some of you in the near future for a job. You should hire them if you get the chance. Despite all this help there are undoubtedly errors of fact and interpretation and infelicities of language for which I alone must accept responsibility.

On a personal level Dimitri Christakis, James Forman, and Evan Westerfield are in disciplines very far from mine. But their friendship has been invaluable. Each is the best in his field, and each ties his professional work to the work of social justice in ways far better than I (though modesty prevents me from immortalizing in print which of us currently holds the title of P. C. Kingpin).

My children, Aubrey, Isha, and Vaughn, have been patient with the writing process, but a little pushy about when it would be done. Both were helpful. Each took the trouble to learn to pronounce "Schleiermacher" correctly, which I appreciate.

Nancy Walsh took my life from black and white to color. The passion, skill, and hard work she puts into making big and important ideas available and exciting to diverse populations is inspirational. She showed me how to make the two charts (Figures 2.1 and 2.2) in Chapter 2, which was important because my computer skills rival those of Schleiermacher.

Finally, this book is dedicated to my parents. It seemed appropriate to dedicate a book on Schleiermacher to them, because like him they have lived their whole lives faithfully in the Reformed tradition, and like him they are the kind of people who threaten to give Christianity a good name.

Introduction

A colleague asked me, "Do we really need another book on Schleiermacher?" I think we do, for at least two reasons. The first reason is the level at which books in English on Schleiermacher are pitched. There are several fine books introducing readers to Schleiermacher, but with one exception they seem to me to be the kind of book that is most easily accessible and useful after one is already fairly familiar with Schleiermacher. Other introductory material available is too simplistic or just inaccurate. One of the appeals of locating an introduction to Schleiermacher in this T&T Clark series is that the books (as they explained to me) are intended to be introductory (and so I assume no exposure to Schleiermacher in order to understand what follows), and yet the books are intended for graduate students and bright undergraduates, so that it is not necessary or desirable to avoid difficult technical issues or dumb the material down in any way. This target audience is the audience I teach, and so I hope I have pitched this introduction to Schleiermacher at a level that is truly introductory yet sophisticated enough to give astute readers some sense of why Schleiermacher is important in the first place.

The second reason for another book on Schleiermacher has to do with coverage. There are many fine monographs on different specific aspects of Schleiermacher's intellectual output, but the general introductions available have focused almost exclusively on his theology. That is not surprising, given that he is most famous as a theologian. It is also not surprising because there tends to be a fair amount of suspicion at English-language universities between those who study religions and theology, and the rest of the faculty. Work on Schleiermacher in the English-speaking world has been confined largely to a kind of theological ghetto of seminaries and divinity schools.

In Germany, Schleiermacher is seen as a broader ranging intellectual, and that is what he is. We have reached the point in the English world where an introduction to Schleiermacher needs to treat other fields in addition to theology. Scholars in various disciplines are examining Schleiermacher's influence, and his usefulness as a resource. I hope to provide an introduction that covers a wider range of disciplines than is currently available.

One added benefit of covering disciplines outside theology is that it is enormously helpful, in interpreting Schleiermacher's theology, to have a background in some of the other work he did. Knowledge of his epistemology, his hermeneutics, his political theory, will allow a better interpretation of his theology, and head off some of the more pervasive misreadings that persist in English secondary literature.

Chapter 1 gives an overview of Schleiermacher's life. I show the historical and personal contexts that influence his work, and try to give an idea of the range of his intellectual passions.

Chapter 2 analyzes Schleiermacher's most basic intellectual commitments. I examine his epistemology, and his theory of history and culture. In doing so I also show the way Schleiermacher divided up the kinds of human knowledge, and the kinds of human activity. This allows us to see how he conceives of his various activities relating to each other.

Chapter 3 is on Schleiermacher's Hermeneutics. He is a pioneer in the modern field of Hermeneutics, and knowing something about how he sees language, and how to interpret language, makes the rest of his thought much more easily accessible.

Chapter 4 is on Schleiermacher as a theorist of religion. He plays a foundational role in the modern study of religion, but in part because he has been read exclusively as a theologian, his contributions have been both misunderstood and maligned. In the humanities it is not possible to advance a discipline without as full and accurate an understanding of the history of the discipline as possible. My hope is that Schleiermacher will be as interesting to non-theological scholars of religion as he is to theologians.

Chapter 5 turns finally to Schleiermacher's theology. It is not possible to cover the full range of the kinds of theology he does, nor the full range of doctrines in his systematic theology. Rather, I focus on the doctrines I think are central to his systematic theology: Christology (his theology is often described as "Christomorphic"), and sin and redemption. I also spend some time on his theological method and the Introduction to *The Christian Faith*, his magnum opus, because these have been the sources of some of the misinterpretations of his theology.

Chapter 6 describes Schleiermacher's political thought, and his activities as a political activist. This aspect of his career may be the most surprising for those with only a passing familiarity with him. Schleiermacher lived at a time when modern nations were taking shape, and when the ways in which we think religions and nations are related to each other were taking shape. He plays an important role in each.

CHAPTER ONE

Life and Times

It is worth spending some time describing the life of Friedrich Daniel Ernst Schleiermacher (1768–1834) in some detail, since his life captures some of the main movements in a tumultuous time in European history. It is his theological and philosophical grappling with these movements that has earned him the epitaph "Father of Modern Theology." Wilhelm Dilthey writes, in his biography of Schleiermacher, "The philosophy of Kant can be completely understood without close attention to his person and his life; Schleiermacher's significance, his world-view, and his work requires a biographical presentation for a fundamental understanding."[1]

Schleiermacher was born and spent most of his life in Prussia, one of the most powerful of the roughly 350 German states (Germany did not unify into a modern nation-state until 1871). Two of the most important things to note about Schleiermacher's Prussia are its religious make-up and its military strength. In 1613 John Sigismund, Elector of Brandenburg (later Brandenburg-Prussia) committed himself to Reformed Christianity, but did not require his subjects also to become Reformed. Most of them remained Lutheran, establishing a dynamic (Reformed ruling family, majority Lutheran population) that continued to Schleiermacher's day.

Prussia's character as an absolutist and militaristic state began under Friedrich Wilhelm (the "Great Elector," who ruled from 1640 to 1688). He took the reins of the Hohenzollern dynasty at a time when the devastations of the Thirty Years' War had threatened its very survival. He concluded that a strong army was the best hope of survival for the small territory without natural frontiers and a shrinking population. Having inherited 5,000 "unruly" troops in 1640, by the time he died he controlled 35,000 well-trained soldiers.[2] He tapped almost the entire landed aristocracy to serve as officers, on the theory that they were used to commanding their serfs. These policies were adopted and extended by Friedrich II (the "Great," who ruled from 1740 to 1786), after whom Schleiermacher is named.

Schleiermacher came from a line of Reformed ministers on both sides. His father Gottlieb Schleyermacher (the son Friedrich changed the spelling) served as a chaplain in Friedrich II's army. He was a rationalist, influenced by the German Enlightenment in the tradition of Gottfried Wilhelm Leibniz (1646–1716) and embodied in Christian Wolff (1679–1754), the leading philosophical figure at the University of Halle, Prussia's flagship university. King Friedrich II was enamored of the Enlightenment, naming his summer estate in Potsdam outside Berlin "Sans Souci" and inviting Voltaire (1694–1778) to live there with him. During this period Kant understands himself to be living in "the age of enlightenment, or the century of Frederick."[3] In 1778 Gottlieb, camped with the troops near the Moravian colony of Gnadenfrei, underwent a pietistic awakening. Pietism, emphasizing religious renewal over doctrine, and a personal relationship with Jesus, was one of the most significant religious and political movements in eighteenth-century Germany. This awakening deeply influenced the course of his family's history.

Gottlieb's father Daniel, Schleiermacher's grandfather, was also a Reformed pastor. He became involved with and preached to a millennialist community headed by the married couple Anna von Büchel and Elias Eller. When Anna died Elias, perhaps in an effort to consolidate his control of the community, accused Daniel of witchcraft, a crime carrying civil penalties. Daniel was forced to flee to the Netherlands in 1749, a scandalous episode that scarred his son Gottlieb (the family later returned to Prussia).

Schleiermacher's mother, Elisabeth Maria Katharina Stubenrauch, was the daughter of a fairly prominent Reformed minister. Her younger brother Samuel Ernst Timotheus Stubenrauch was a preacher and professor, and he played a significant role in Schleiermacher's life.

Schleiermacher remained close to his younger brother Johann Carl, later a dentist, and especially his older sister Charlotte. Charlotte lived with and ran Schleiermacher's household for significant portions of their adulthood. (Schleiermacher's small physical stature is attributed to his being dropped at a young age by Charlotte, an accident that also resulted in a slight hunchback.)

Because of their father's peripatetic career the Schleiermacher children received very little regular schooling. Their parents decided to enroll them in a Moravian boarding school, which they chose because of its reputation for piety and excellent pedagogy. After an initial interview at the school in Niesky, the Moravians cast lots to make a final decision on admission (thus placing it in God's hands), and decided to accept the children, first Friedrich and Carl, later Charlotte. Entering the school at the age of fourteen and a half, Friedrich spent four years, critical to his personal growth, with the Moravians (at Niesky 1783–85 and 1785–87 at the Moravian seminary at Barby). He would not see his parents again. His mother died at age 47 a few months after his matriculation. He carried on a lively correspondence with his father. Gottlieb remarried in 1785, and he had three more daughters. The eldest, Anne Maria Louise (called "Nanny") ran Schleiermacher's household for a time in Halle and Berlin, and in 1817 she married Ernst Moritz Arndt, the historian, writer, and perhaps most famously agitator for a German constitutional nation, a cause also dear to Schleiermacher's heart.

Schleiermacher received an excellent education among the Moravians, and just as important he experienced deeply the moving, community-based commitment and emotion of pietistic religion, complete with a dated conversion. He writes, in his *Speeches on Religion* (1799): "Religion was the maternal womb in whose holy darkness my young life was nourished and prepared for the world still closed to it." But Schleiermacher also admits to a skeptical streak that had always run through him. The quote from the *Speeches* continues:

> Religion helped me when I began to examine the ancestral faith and to purify my heart of the rubble of primitive times. It remained with me when God and immortality disappeared before my doubting eyes.[4]

At the seminary in Barby he formed a reading club with some close friends, sneaking in and discussing works by Kant and Goethe among others, works that were forbidden by the Brethren precisely because they might work against the community's carefully cultivated piety.

In a letter dated January 21, 1787, Schleiermacher makes a confession to his father that he had been working up to for some time:[5]

> Faith is the regalia of the Godhead, you say. Alas! Dearest father, if you believe that without this faith no one can attain to salvation in the next world, nor to tranquility in this—and such, I know, is your belief—oh! then pray to God to grant it to me, for to me it is now lost. I cannot believe that he who called himself the Son of Man was the true, eternal God; I cannot believe that his death was a vicarious atonement.

His father replies that his son "has crucified Christ, disturbed his late mother's rest, and made his stepmother weep." He disowns Friedrich: "I must, for you no longer worship the God of your father, no longer kneel at the same altar with him." He tempers this harsh response in the last line of his letter: "I can add no more except the assurance that with sorrowing and heavy heart, I remain your deeply compassionate and loving father."

The story does not end there, for the Schleiermacher family or for the history of theology. Father and son eventually reconcile. Though Schleiermacher is asked to leave the seminary, his father agrees to support a short period of study at the University of Halle. In 1802 Schleiermacher returned to the Moravian community for a visit, famously writing:

> Here it was for the first time I awoke to the consciousness of the relations of man to a higher world. . . . Here it was that that mystic tendency developed itself, which has been of so much importance to me, and has supported and carried me through all the storms of skepticism. . . . And I may say, that after all that I have passed though, I have become a Herrnhuter [Moravian] again, only of a higher order.

It is probably fortunate that these remarks were not made publicly to the Moravians—I am not sure how the "higher order" comment would have been received. But we are in a position to step back from this biographical narrative (there is more I will want to add shortly) and make explicit some of the major intellectual themes we will be covering in the following chapters, themes that shape Schleiermacher's work into such a significant contribution.

First, in Schleiermacher's comments about religion being a "maternal womb," about the religion he learned with the Moravians carrying him through his period of doubt, and his remark that he is a Moravian again "of a higher order," we see the sharp distinction he makes between religion and theology. Religion is an experience of redemption found in community. Theology is reflection on and articulation of that experience. In Schleiermacher's personal history we see recapitulated the cultural history of the move from Reformation Bible-based orthodoxy through the critical epistemological challenges of the Enlightenment. Schleiermacher's ability to come out to the other side of this history with his religion intact but with a new way of doing theology is what makes him so significant in the history of theology. When Schleiermacher writes to his father that he can no longer believe in the orthodox two-natures doctrine of Christ or the vicarious atonement, we see, as B. A. Gerrish aptly puts it, "that what Schleiermacher lost was not his faith in Christ but his first understanding of it."[6] His move to place modern theology on the foundation of experience, an experience not challenged by Enlightenment epistemologies the same way that foundations of Scripture and reason were challenged by those epistemologies, and his ability to understand that experience and articulate it in such a way that this articulation does not duck these epistemological challenges posed by the Enlightenment but instead grasps and even embraces them, is precisely what makes Schleiermacher the "Father of Modern Theology."

We will need to say a lot more about the nature of this experience, and how Schleiermacher articulates the work effected by Jesus and what is meant by salvation. In doing so we will also have a lot more to say about how Schleiermacher thinks about communities and what this means for churches and for modern nations. In explaining how Schleiermacher conceives of the relationship of individuals to communities, we will also need to say more about his theory of language (Hermeneutics) and Philosophical Ethics (by which Schleiermacher means a theory of history and culture).

From Barby, Schleiermacher went to Halle from 1787–89. Halle was the center both of the German Enlightenment (Christian Wolff was professor there) and German Pietism. There he lived with his Uncle Stubenrauch (his mother's brother), who was professor of Church History and Holy Antiquity at the Reformed Gymnasium, and guest professor at the University. At Halle, Schleiermacher apparently spent more time reading on his own than attending lectures. His engagement with Kant deepened greatly, and while he always had a somewhat critical stance vis-à-vis Kant, Schleiermacher was not an enthusiastic follower of Johann August Eberhard (a follower of Wolff and one of Kant's most prominent critics). In 1789 Schleiermacher followed his uncle to the small town of Drossen, where the latter had accepted an appointment as pastor. Schleiermacher was not happy in Drossen, a pattern we will see repeated in his young adulthood—he tended to thrive in culturally vibrant contexts, and felt deprived to the point that it affected his physical health in smaller places out of the leading currents of intellectual, cultural, and political events. He spent his time in Drossen, as he had in Halle, writing philosophical essays and sketches, many of which would be important for his later work. Some of the essays Schleiermacher worked on in Halle and Drossen show his continuing engagement with Kant: "On the Highest Good"; "Notes on Kant: The Critique of Practical Reason"; "Discourse on Freedom [*Freiheitsgespräch*]"; "On Freedom."

He showed no great interest in religious or theological matters at this time, though he did travel to Berlin in April and May of 1790 and passed his first round of theology exams. (He scored good and very good marks in all exams except "Dogmatics," for which he received a grade of "passable," thereby offering hope to generations of later theology students.)

Having passed his first set of exams, Schleiermacher was eligible for employment. His Uncle Stubenrauch pressed his old friend Friedrich Samuel Gottfried Sack, court preacher and church official, to help find Schleiermacher a position. Pulpits were few and far between, but Sack did arrange for Schleiermacher to serve as tutor to the family of Count Friedrich Dohna, head of one of Prussia's leading noble families. The Dohnas lived on a beautiful estate in East Prussia. They had twelve children, eight of whom still lived at home while Schleiermacher was tutor. The two oldest sons, Alexander and Wilhelm Graf zu Dohna, with whom Schleiermacher became good friends, were studying in Berlin and Königsberg.

Schleiermacher lived with the Dohnas from 1790 to 1793, greatly enjoying his time with them. The family circle was close and warm. He had the opportunity to preach occasionally, and experienced a religious revitalization. He fell secretly in love with one of the Dohna daughters, Frederika. In May 1791 he made a one and a half day trip to Königsberg, where he met with several faculty members, including a half hour conversation with Kant (neither made a huge impression on the other). He departed the family on friendly terms, though there were some tensions during his time with them that apparently led to his departure. Count Dohna, despite his lack of pedagogical gifts, sometimes appeared unannounced in Schleiermacher's lessons and took over instruction. More importantly, perhaps, was the Count's discomfort with Schleiermacher's sympathy for the French Revolution. These political differences became unbridgeable with the beheading of Louis XVI in January 1793.

Schleiermacher, at loose ends, once again found employment through the efforts of Sack. The 1700s was a century of pedagogical reform, and Prussia's first institute dedicated to creating a professionalized and reform-minded work force of teachers was founded in Berlin by Friedrich Gedike. Sack placed Schleiermacher on the faculty of Gedike's "pedagogical seminary." It was during the winter of 1793–94 that Schleiermacher engaged the philosophy of Baruch Spinoza (1632–77). Spinoza had long been reviled and dismissed as Europe's most dangerous philosopher, a man whose system led inevitably to pantheism and determinism. In the 1780s the famous "Pantheism Controversy" broke out in German intellectual circles, initiated by the debate between Friedrich Heinrich Jacobi (1743–1819) and Moses Mendelssohn (1729–86) over whether or not Gotthold Ephraim Lessing (1729–81), one of the leading lights of the German Enlightenment, had become a "Spinozist" just before his death. In the course of the controversy German intellectuals engaged Spinoza directly and seriously for the first time, and his influence and reputation ascended rapidly. Schleiermacher was not one of the elite few who had direct access to Spinoza's writings, but he studied carefully Jacobi's presentation of Spinoza in *On the Teachings of Spinoza in Letters to Herr Mendelssohn*. Spinoza's thought influenced Schleiermacher's life greatly, both in terms of his intellectual development and, as we will see, in very practical ways as well. During this time Schleiermacher worked out manuscripts on "Spinozism" and "Short Presentation of the Spinozistic System."[7]

In February 1794 the elderly preacher in Landsberg, Schumann, asked for an assistant pastor. Sack placed Schleiermacher in the position, but first Schleiermacher had to pass his second round of theology exams, which he did in March 1794. It was in Landsberg that Schleiermacher learned of the death of his father, Gottlieb, too late to participate in the funeral. During this time Sack, an admirer of English Enlightenment preaching, asked Schleiermacher to co-translate the sermons of Hugo Blair, which appeared in 1795. In June 1795 Pastor Schumann died. Despite the desire of the congregation to have Schleiermacher take over his post, Sack somewhat surprisingly wrote to him that it was "probable, that you will not be staying in Landsberg."[8]

Instead Schleiermacher was appointed as preacher at the Charité Hospital in Berlin. The hospital, founded by Friedrich I to treat victims of the plague, had been converted to a home for the elderly and sick when the plague passed. During Schleiermacher's tenure it had 680 beds in 8 departments, and had a large indigent clientele. While Schleiermacher was in Berlin, from 1796 to 1802, he became an active participant in the early Romantic circle, an association that profoundly shaped his thought and expression. The Romantics were the leading edge of European art and culture. They were profoundly influenced by the "Sturm und Drang" movement of Goethe. In Berlin the movement centered on literary salons, the three most important of which were run by Henriette Herz, Sara von Grotthuß, and Rahel Levin (later Rahel Varnhagen). Schleiermacher's entrance to Henriette Herz's salon came in the form of an invitation on December 30, 1796 from Alexander Dohna (son of his former employer) to join him there for dinner. Henriette was the wife of Markus Herz, a doctor and author named by Kant as one of his favorite students, friend of the deceased Lessing, and appointed by Friedrich Wilhelm II as professor of Philosophy. Henriette was herself quite brilliant, speaking many languages and pursuing important literary projects. Her salon included Berlin's leading intellectuals and authors:

the Humboldt brothers (Wilhelm and Alexander), Brinckmann, Tieck, Kleist, Dorothea and Henriette Mendelssohn, Alexander and Wilhelm Dohna, and from his arrival in Berlin in 1797 on, Friedrich Schlegel.

Compared to others in Herz's salon in Berlin, Schleiermacher was not so gifted a writer of fine literature (indeed, readers of his *Christmas Eve Dialogue*, an important work theologically, will not mistake him for one of Romanticism's great writers of fiction). Nevertheless, he was acknowledged as the most brilliant conversationalist of them all (an important role for a circle that valued what it called *Symphilosophie*, or the practice of thinking and writing as a group rather than as individuals). Friedrich Schlegel wrote of Schleiermacher that "what Goethe is to poetry, and Fichte is to philosophy, Schleiermacher is to humanity," and Bettina Brentano von Arnim wrote that "he was not the greatest man [*Mann*] of his time, he was the greatest human being [*Mensch*]."[9] Henriette Herz wrote to Brinckmann, "Schleiermacher is a rare appearance to me . . . so much understanding, so much knowledge, so full of love and yet so tender, so totally beautiful a nature [*Gemüths*]. If ever something be made of me, so it will happen through him, who takes so much trouble to make something of me."[10]

While it is notoriously difficult to define German Romanticism, one thing that most attempts have in common is the central role played by Friedrich Schlegel. Schleiermacher wrote to his sister Charlotte, after meeting Schlegel:

> He is a young man of twenty five years, of such wide ranging knowledge, that one cannot conceive how it is possible with such youth to know so much, of an original spirit, who here where there is so much spirit and talent still surpasses all by a wide margin. . . . In short, since my closer friendship with him begins as it were for my existence in the philosophical and literary worlds a new period.[11]

Schleiermacher and Schlegel were roommates for a period of 18 months (December 1797 to August 1799) and became so close that their friends referred to them as a married couple. It was the instigation of Schlegel that led to the event typically taken to mark the beginning of modern liberal Protestant theology. Schlegel, with Alexander and Wilhelm Dohna, Henriette Herz, and Dorothea

Veit, surprised Schleiermacher, at work at his writing table in his apartment, at 10 a.m. on his twenty-ninth birthday, with chocolates, cake, a watch, gloves, a wineglass, and perfume. In toasting and roasting Schleiermacher Schlegel said, "29 years old and nothing yet accomplished! . . . I want something written this year."[12]

The result of this challenge is Schleiermacher's *On Religion: Speeches to Its Cultured Despisers*, published in 1799 (hereafter referred to as the *Speeches*). It is not hard to read in Schleiermacher's circle, made up largely of rationalist Jews and post-Christian libertines, some puzzlement that their close friend could be a Reformed preacher at the same time. Schleiermacher's *Speeches* is his response to their puzzlement. In this classic work Schleiermacher began where much of his audience was (the cultured despisers of religion are precisely his Romantic circle). He argues that what they take religion to be (priests and rituals) is not religion, and furthermore what they find most important (the experience of the infinite in the finite, which leads to creative insight) is exactly what religion is. By the fifth and final speech Schleiermacher has hoped to lead them to the view that this experience is best cultivated in community, and the community founded to cultivate it most effectively is the Christian church. (It is worth noting that through Schleiermacher the leaders of all three Berlin salons, Henriette Herz, Dorothea Veit, and Rahel Varnhagen, eventually converted from a rationalist Judaism to an emotive Christianity. Friedrich Schlegel, after drifting away from Schleiermacher, eventually became Roman Catholic.)

About the *Speeches* I will have much more to say in later chapters as I examine Schleiermacher's theology and philosophy. Here I want simply to point out that the *Speeches* was one of the important factors causing Sack, Schleiermacher's ecclesiastical superior and the man who had so carefully looked out for Schleiermacher's early career, to bring Schleiermacher's time in Berlin to an end. Sack moved Schleiermacher to a small parish in what Schleiermacher considered to be the backwater of Stolp, a small town on the Baltic Sea in Pomerania, a bitter move for Schleiermacher.

On Sack's reading, the *Speeches* preached not Christianity but a form of pantheism. Sack was concerned that Schleiermacher, like Fichte before him (who had been fired from his job at the University of Jena in 1799), was espousing a position too close to Spinoza's. While I will try to show in Chapter 5 that this is not a particularly nuanced reading, it is true that in one important passage of the *Speeches* Schleiermacher heaps praises on the dreaded Spinoza:

> Respectfully offer up with me a lock of hair to the manes of the holy rejected Spinoza! The high world spirit permeated him, the infinite was his beginning and end, the universe his only and eternal love; in holy innocence and deep humility he was reflected in the eternal world and saw how he too was its most lovable mirror; he was full of religion and full of holy spirit; for this reason he also stands there alone and unequaled, master in his art but elevated above the profane guild, without disciples and without rights of citizenship.[13]

Sack determined that Schleiermacher, for his own good, had to be removed from the influence of Romanticism. (I should point out here that "Romanticism" takes its name, not from any connection to the genre of what we call today Romance literature, but from the word for imaginative literature, especially the novel, the German word for which is *Roman*. This quintessentially modern art form was reshaped by Goethe's novels [*Bildungsromanne*], and was taken as a model of creativity and individual authentic development.) The Romantic influence threatened not only Schleiermacher's theology but, from Sack's perspective, Schleiermacher's morality. Part of the Romantic project was not merely to challenge the reigning literary and philosophical forms of the day, but also to criticize what they saw as the desiccated and deadening social arrangements of Germany. In particular, marriage was seen as an unequal and limiting institution. Friedrich Schlegel shocked society by pursuing an affair with Dorothea Veit, a married woman, and then writing about it in a scandalous thinly veiled autobiographical novel, *Lucinde*. Schleiermacher won himself no friends in the church hierarchy by defending this novel in print (he published *Confidential Letters on Schlegel's Lucinde* in 1801). Furthermore, Schleiermacher's own love life was suspect. He fell in love with Eleonore Grunow in 1799, a woman trapped in a loveless marriage to an older Lutheran minister. While Schleiermacher did not follow the same route as Schlegel, he did court Eleonore publicly and try to convince her to divorce her husband. In 1801 he confronted the Reverend Grunow about his (mis)treatment of his wife. Better, Sack thought, to appoint Schleiermacher as court chaplain in Stolp. Schleiermacher left Berlin in 1802.[14]

Schleiermacher's time in Stolp was the unhappiest of his life. He felt he was in exile in the town with 4,000 inhabitants, 250 of whom made up the Reformed community. Eleonore Grunow's continued indecisiveness tormented him. He became close friends with Ehrenfried von Willich, a candidate in theology 10 years younger. Von Willich, serving as house tutor in a noble household, as Schleiermacher had done, also found himself in love with a married woman (Johanna Herz, younger sister of Henriette Herz, married to Simon Herz, a Jewish doctor). They had much in common. Schleiermacher also complained to von Willich about his growing distance from Friedrich Schlegel. In spring 1803 Eleonore finally made a definitive break, writing to Schleiermacher that she would not leave her husband. He was devastated. Eleonore eventually relented, dragging out their relationship until 1806.

His depression, however, did not prevent him from working. Among other projects, Schleiermacher completed the first volume of his translation of Plato's dialogues, which appeared in the spring of 1804. The project to translate all the dialogues was originally a joint project with Friedrich Schlegel, but Schlegel was notoriously better at starting projects than finishing them. Schleiermacher published most of the corpus by 1809, completing the project by 1828 (with the exceptions of the *Timaeus* and the *Laws*). In the chronology Schleiermacher proposes for the dialogues and in the way he translates them, Schleiermacher is considered to be the first to break free of Neoplatonic assumptions. His chronology was based on the inner logic of each dialogue and on linguistic evidence, and on a supposition about the development of Plato's thought. With a couple of exceptions Schleiermacher's suppositions have proven to be correct. We will see, in our discussion of Schleiermacher's Hermeneutics, the philosophical basis for Schleiermacher's translation work. His translation continues to be the benchmark for German translations of Plato.[15]

Schleiermacher also published in 1804 *Two Unanticipated Opinions in the Matter of the Protestant Church Chiefly in Connection with the Prussian State*. In these essays Schleiermacher argued that the continued separation of the Lutheran and Reformed confessions in Prussia was not useful. Most congregants no longer knew the dogmatic basis of the separation, with the result that people clung to external words and formalities. This bred superstition and a partisan spirit. Schleiermacher proposed that, rather than trying to create a creed that somehow split the dogmatic differences down the middle, it would be enough to create a liturgy that allowed congregants from the two confessions to celebrate the Lord's Supper together.[16]

Though Schleiermacher sometimes feared he would remain in Stolp forever, the wider world had not forgotten about him. In October 1803 he received a letter from Goethe. At the beginning of 1804 another letter arrived, this one from Heinrich Eberhard Gottlob Paulus (1761–1851), a famous rationalist and biblical critic. Paulus had been on the faculty at the University of Jena when Fichte had been let go because of the "Atheism Controversy" (another fight over Spinoza). Along with Friedrich Wilhelm Joseph Schelling (1775–1854), Paulus was now on the faculty at the University of Würzburg. Paulus was writing with an invitation to join the faculty. Schleiermacher hesitated for two reasons: he did not want to take a position that did not include preaching responsibilities, and he did not want to leave Prussia. But seeing little chance for advancement within Prussia, he finally accepted the invitation.

King Friedrich Wilhelm III (reigned 1797–1840), learning of Schleiermacher's imminent departure, directed his commission to find Schleiermacher a position within Prussia. The King was motivated by two factors: he did not want to lose one of Prussia's brightest young intellectual lights to another German state. And the King, a devout Reformed Christian, had a deep desire to take communion with his wife, Queen Louise, a devout Lutheran. He therefore had a strong interest in unifying the two confessions in Prussia, and in the wake of Schleiermacher's arguments in the *Two Unanticipated Opinions* saw Schleiermacher as an important ally in this quest.

The King's first idea was to find Schleiermacher a preaching position in Berlin. But by May 1804 the King instead created for Schleiermacher a position on the theology faculty at the University of Halle (the first Reformed position at the Lutheran University) and combined this position with the post of University preacher.[17]

Before arriving in Halle Schleiermacher took a vacation on the beloved island of Rüge, in the Baltic Sea. His friend Ehrenfried von Willich lived there. Among the other participants in this vacation was Henriette von Mühlenfels. She and von Willich fell in love during the vacation, and they were married just a few weeks later.

Schleiermacher arrived in Halle on October 10, 1804. He taught there for four semesters. Halle's faculty was largely Lutheran, and Schleiermacher's appointment was by no means welcome to many. One issue to be resolved was where the academic worship services, with Schleiermacher as (Reformed) University preacher, were to be held. The presbytery did not turn over the Reformed Cathedral. The School Church was being used by Prussia's army as an armory. After much bureaucratic finagling the School Church was renovated, and Schleiermacher entered the pulpit as University preacher for the first time on August 3, 1806.

In the classroom Schleiermacher was a generalist. He lectured two times on "Encyclopedia," a discipline that laid out an overview of theological study (published in 1811 as the *Brief Outline on the Study of Theology*, a plan for theological preparation that most denominational seminaries still largely follow. I will describe this book in Chapter 5). He also lectured on Dogmatics, Ethics, New Testament, and he held a class on Method in Church History as well.[18] In summer 1805 he lectured on Hermeneutics. A course on Practical Theology was planned for his fifth semester, a semester that did not take place for reasons I will explain shortly. An important lacuna to note is the lack of any course on the Old Testament. At this time Schleiermacher also wrote an important work of New Testament Criticism, "On the So-Called First Letter of Paul to Timothy," as well as a work on Ethics, "Brouillon on Ethics. 1805."

Schleiermacher's most significant theological publication in the two years he was in Halle was *Christmas Eve: A Dialogue on the Incarnation* (1806). The book was written at a feverish pace in December 1805. The inspiration for the dialogue came suddenly to Schleiermacher in the wake of a flute concert by the blind virtuoso Friedrich Ludwig Dulon. Schleiermacher's hope was to have the book ready to give as a Christmas present, but on Christmas Eve he was still hard at work on it. It appeared in the first days of 1806.

Christmas Eve is an excellent point of entry for newcomers to Schleiermacher's theology. His previous major theological work, the *Speeches*, was addressed to literary and philosophical elites, and its language alternates between technical philosophy and rapturous Romantic poetics. The *Speeches* began with the concept of religion in general and then moved toward Christianity. *Christmas Eve*, in contrast, begins with a depiction of a typical middle-class German Christmas celebration. In it we see Schleiermacher's famous Christology "from below." Rather than starting with Scripture or doctrinal statements or creeds, *Christmas Eve* takes as its starting point Christian experience. While the men at the party debate the finer points of theology, almost killing the party, the music provided by young Sofie, the stories told by the women, and the gifts given are a kind of manifestation and showing of the effects of the Redeemer's presence on earth. This turn to experience as the starting point, argued for in the *Speeches* but shown in *Christmas Eve*, is the touchstone of Schleiermacher's theology.

On October 14, 1806 French troops, led by Napoleon, crushed the famous Prussian army in the battles of Jena and Auerstädt. Most of Prussia was occupied, the King and his court fled to Königsberg on the far northeast coast of Prussia, and agreed to onerous reparations. The defeat was more than simply a military devastation. Prussia's place in Europe had been established by the outsized and widely respected army it had been building up since the reign of the Great Elector in the mid-seventeenth century. Prussia's very identity, and the future of Protestantism (the other major German state was the Catholic Austria) were called into question.

Napoleon entered Halle on October 17, 1806. Schleiermacher had French officers billeted in his apartment, his watch and money were confiscated. Napoleon shut down the university on October 20. The church where Schleiermacher conducted worship was used to store grain. Schleiermacher remained in Halle, though jobless, until December 31, 1807. Upon learning that Napoleon had placed Halle in the Kingdom of Westphalia, ruled by Napoleon's brother Jerome, Schleiermacher wrote to a friend, "I cannot accommodate myself to this government and must live under a German prince, so long as there is one."[19] He left for Berlin.

When Schleiermacher left Halle for Berlin he found among his papers an essay, "Occasional Thoughts on the University in the German Sense." He revised and finished it, and it was published in spring 1808. Since the closing of the University of Halle, Prussia's flagship university, only the Universities of Königsberg and Frankfurt an der Oder remained to the Prussian monarchy. The government began plans for a new university in Berlin, partly as a way of preserving Prussia's identity, at least intellectually if not as a state power. Schleiermacher was overlooked in the early planning stages of the university. Eventually Wilhelm von Humboldt was given responsibility for founding the university, and Schleiermacher was brought in as one of the planning team and its secretary. When Humboldt left this position after 16 months to become ambassador in Vienna, Schleiermacher and his colleagues were left to carry on the process. The university now bears Humboldt's name. When it opened in 1810 it followed the outline found in Schleiermacher's essay fairly closely.

Schleiermacher argues, in his essay, that a university should stand between two other kinds of institutions, the Gymnasium and the institutes for specialists (there were, in Prussia, medical schools, veterinary schools, military academies, etc. not associated with any university). Whereas in the Gymnasiums students learned content, and in the institutes specialists pursued research, the university was the place where love of learning was awakened in the students. Faculty therefore had a dual responsibility: to do research and to teach. The unifying discipline was to be philosophy, in which everyone should have a grounding. Students also could study in one of three professional schools: law, medicine, and theology.

As Prussia moved from a state relying primarily on personal acquaintances of the king for governance to one relying on a professional class of trained administrators (not an easy transition under King Wilhelm Friedrich III), the demand for university graduates grew. Yet the goal of the university, in Schleiermacher's essay and in the university's plan, was not merely professional education but more importantly *Bildung*, a German word that can be translated somewhat inadequately as "education" and as "development." (Goethe's novels are *Bildungsromanne* in which a young character, through a series of intense ups and downs, matures into a distinct personality out of, but developed from, the character's personality at the start of the process.) In other words, through instruction, study, and most importantly conversation, the students at Humboldt's university were to be offered the opportunity to develop into full and distinct human beings.

Schleiermacher argued that, because these fully developed and trained graduates were precisely what was most needed by the state, the state should support the university. At the same time, because professors could not pursue their research under state pressure for immediate applicability, nor could they guide student development with outside interference, the state should not meddle in the internal affairs of the university.

The University of Berlin played an important role in the history of higher education. It became the model of a modern research university. We see in it, in early form, many of the features we take for granted as parts of the American university experience (I am less familiar with universities in the United Kingdom). Students are exposed to some sort of liberal arts courses before specializing in a field (not all study philosophy but core courses or distribution requirements are intended to fulfill this goal). The goal is not merely professional training but exposure to a set of disciplines and experiences that are intended to enrich and edify. Faculty both teach and do research, and their research is protected by tenure or other forms of academic freedom. In the United States, Johns Hopkins (1876) and The University of Chicago (1892) were founded largely on the Berlin model, as well as Cornell (1865) to some extent. The University of Michigan was reorganized on the Berlin model in 1852. Other, older colleges like Harvard and Yale quickly retooled themselves on this model to keep pace. Yale was the first American university to offer a Ph.D. (in 1861). Prior to that most Americans with Ph.D.s earned them in Germany.[20]

In May 1809 Schleiermacher married Henriette von Willich, widow of his close friend Ehrenfried von Willich, who had died in 1807. Henriette had two young children, and in the wake of her husband's death Schleiermacher had entered into a correspondence with the young widow that was, at the start, pastoral. In addition to Henriette's two children she and Schleiermacher had four more children. Their only son, Nathanael, died in 1829 at the age of 9. Schleiermacher's graveside sermon, in addition to being almost unbearably moving, is an accessible point of entry to some key aspects of his theology.[21]

Henriette Schleiermacher befriended Karoline Fischer, a medium who, in hypnotic trances, conversed with the dead. She exercised great influence over several of the Schleiermacher children. Eventually Henriette took in Fischer's daughter, Luise, in effect unifying the two households. Despite Schleiermacher's distaste for this kind of spiritualism, he remained true to his commitment to the importance of giving freedom to individuals to develop in their own way and he thereby largely put up with his wife's beliefs and Fischer's influence in his household.

In June 1809, having served the customary year as intern following the death of its previous pastor, Schleiermacher was installed as Reformed pastor of Trinity Church (*Dreifaltigkeitskirche*). The church, founded in 1739 by King Friedrich Wilhelm I for both Lutherans and Reformed, had a membership of 12,000. Schleiermacher remained in that pastorate and pulpit until his death.

When the University of Berlin opened in 1810 Schleiermacher was dean of the Theological Faculty, Fichte was the first rector. Schleiermacher served as rector in 1815/16. Schleiermacher was also appointed to the Berlin Academy of Sciences, where he served as secretary (president) of the philosophical section for many years.

At the University of Berlin, Schleiermacher lectured on Hermeneutics, various aspects of Church History and New Testament, Dialectic, Philosophical Ethics, Christian Ethics, Theory of the State, Practical Theology, Psychology, Pedagogy, Aesthetics, and History of Philosophy (the list is not exhaustive). His most important publications include *Brief Outline of the Study of Theology* (1811, second edition 1830), *The Christian Faith* (first edition 1820/21; second edition 1830/31), and *On the Glaubenslehre: Two Letters to Dr. Lücke* (1829), an open letter defending the first edition of *The Christian Faith* and explaining the revisions in the second. *The Christian Faith*[22] is typically ranked as one of the most important Christian systematic theologies, along with Thomas's *Summa Theologiae*, Calvin's *Institutes of the Christian Religion*, and Barth's *Church Dogmatics*.

During the war years 1806–13 Schleiermacher was associated with, though he apparently never officially joined, a secret group known as the Union of Virtue (*Tugendbund*), whose mission was to plan for a popular uprising against the French in various German states, and coordinate this uprising with the government in Königsberg. On August 20, 1808 Schleiermacher undertook a dangerous mission as messenger from the group to the court in Königsberg (the group apparently thought that a traveling pastor would raise fewer suspicions among the French occupiers than other possible messengers). Schleiermacher arrived in Königsberg on August 25. There he met with the Queen and crown prince, First Minister Baron von Stein, and the King's Chief of Staff and

Minister of War. The King asked to hear him preach, which he did on September 4. The mission cannot be counted a great success. Schleiermacher had worked out a complicated encryption device for correspondence home. Schleiermacher had a piece of paper with an oddly shaped hole torn in it. He laid this paper on top of a piece of stationary, wrote his message, then removed the paper and filled in words around the message to make the letter appear to be a normal letter. The group in Berlin had a piece of paper with the same shaped hole torn in it, to lay on top of the letter and reveal the message. The system proved too cumbersome. His friends wrote to him, after receiving his first letter, "The exemplariness of your letter did not want to shine on any of us, at least it suffered from the consequences of immoderation."[23] Schleiermacher then tried using invisible ink, with no better results.

I will have more to say about Schleiermacher's political thought and activity and its connection to his theology in Chapter 6. All his efforts were in the service of a reformist model of community that allowed for the free development (*Bildung*) of its members, and the kind of committed participation such members could bring in forming a healthy organic community. Though the King hesitantly tapped this reform movement in his struggles against the French and had promised his subjects a constitution, when Napoleon was defeated in 1815 a period of reaction set in across Europe and in Prussia. The constitution was never forthcoming. King Friedrich Wilhelm III signed the Karlsbad Decrees of September 20, 1819, a reactionary agreement among German states to defend monarchical absolutism[24] and root out "subversive" (liberal) tendencies in the universities and in the press. Schleiermacher continued his activities, but now he and the King worked at cross-purposes. Schleiermacher frequently had government spies in his lecture hall and in his pews, and was once threatened with exile.

In 1814 the King established a commission to take up again the project of unifying the Prussian confessions. Schleiermacher attacked the commission because such unification, he argued, could not be by order of a civil authority but had to grow out of the community itself. In October 1817, by order of the King, the confessions did unify, and Schleiermacher with his Lutheran colleague Philip Marheineke celebrated communion together in the Nicolai Church on October 30, in commemoration of the 300th anniversary of the Reformation. Schleiermacher edited the new hymnal for the unified church, and his great systematic theology, *The Christian Faith* (the subject of Chapter 5) is a theology written for the unified church.

Schleiermacher and the King again clashed, beginning in 1821, when the King attempted to bring order to the diverse liturgies in the churches in Prussia by taking up the pen and writing his own liturgy. Once again Schleiermacher objected to the imposition of an order of worship by a civil authority. When the King appealed to the authority of Luther to defend his liturgy (it was modeled on Luther's liturgy) Schleiermacher pointed out the irony of an appeal to tradition by a Protestant. It is in this context that Schleiermacher famously wrote, "The Reformation still goes on!"[25]

In the last days of January 1834, Schleiermacher suffered from a bad cold. It quickly developed into pneumonia. He died on February 12, 1834. After a service at his house an honor guard of students carried his casket to the cemetery. The King rode in the first of 100 carriages in the procession, for which it is estimated that 20,000 Berliners turned out. While this book will focus almost exclusively on Schleiermacher's intellectual work, it is likely that the affection for Schleiermacher that drew most of these mourners was based on Schleiermacher's preaching. His most widely used texts in his lifetime were the hymnal he edited and his published sermons. And that would have pleased him, for of all the honorifics granted him in his life, the title of which he was most proud was "servant of the word."

CHAPTER TWO

Schleiermacher's Worldview

In this chapter I want to lay out some of Schleiermacher's basic intellectual ways of operating. While Schleiermacher is most famous as a theologian, he made significant contributions to many fields that lie outside theology. One of the contributions I hope to make in this book is to provide an account of these contributions. Other introductions have largely stuck to his theology proper. But in today's academy Schleiermacher is not confined to the theological disciplines. His work in other fields is important in its own right. A proper introduction to Schleiermacher can no longer retain a sole focus on theology. These various contributions are related to each other by his systematic cast of mind, and all stem from his basic intellectual commitments. In addition to covering some of the intellectual territory Schleiermacher covered, one benefit of this chapter is to bring some order to the discussion of these various fields of endeavor in subsequent chapters. Schleiermacher provided an architectonic of human knowledge. He also provided a way of schematizing the various fields of human activity in such a way that we can see how they relate to each other. Having this architectonic and this schematization at our fingertips will help us place the discussions in later chapters into proper relation to each other.

Furthermore, his work in epistemology, theory of history and culture, and hermeneutics are enormously helpful in making some of his theological decisions clear, and wading through the controversies those decisions provoked. Some of the errors in interpreting Schleiermacher's theology come from a lack of awareness of how he relates religion and theology to other activities and disciplines. Other errors stem from lack of awareness of his epistemology, theory of history and culture, and hermeneutics. Keeping these in mind will rule out some of the readings of his theology that, unfortunately, have dominated English secondary literature.

In this chapter I will begin with his theory of knowledge, focusing on his lectures on Dialectic. These lectures are famously opaque and the subject of ongoing debate in the secondary literature. The best way in to them, in my opinion, is to see what issues were most pressing in Schleiermacher's own generation. So I begin with a rehearsal of some of Hume's and Kant's philosophies. I will then characterize broadly what Schleiermacher's generation perceived to be some of the major problems with this Enlightenment legacy. To do this I rely on Charles Taylor's perceptive analysis of these issues.[1] We can then see how Schleiermacher positions himself in relation to these same issues.

I then turn to his philosophy of history and culture, found primarily in his lectures on Philosophical Ethics. In Chapter 3 I will discuss his Hermeneutics. In all of these discussions the theme of language is front and center. Schleiermacher's arguments about humans as fundamentally linguistic beings, and the ways in which he analyzes language, continue to impact the philosophical and theological worlds to this day.

Kant

In an oft-quoted passage, Kant writes in his *Critique of Practical Reason* (1788), "Two things fill the mind with ever new and increasing admiration and awe the more enduringly reflection is occupied with them: **the starry heavens above me and the moral law within me.**"[2] These two things can stand for two of Kant's major philosophical concerns: how we know the world around us, and in particular how we can have secure scientific knowledge of it; and how we know and can do the right thing. These two concerns are connected, as we will see in a minute, but I will start with the first.

Kant's first critique, *The Critique of Pure Reason* (1781), inaugurated a revolution in epistemology (how we know what we know) and philosophy. As Kant writes in his *Prolegomena to Any Future Metaphysics* (1783), which he wrote to clarify some of the arguments of the first critique, it was Hume's argument about causation that "awakened [Kant] from [his] dogmatic slumber and gave a completely different direction to [his] researches" in philosophy.[3] Hume had argued that the idea of cause, without which humans could not function and could know very little, was not an a priori idea. We did not know cause before experience. One could not logically work out ahead of time that lightning would necessarily cause thunder. But neither was cause a matter of a posteriori knowledge (after experience). We experienced lightning, and then we experienced thunder, but there was no third experience between the two that we could see, hear, taste, touch, or smell that was the experience of cause. If we neither thought cause logically apart from experience, the way we show that the sum of the square of the two sides of a right triangle equals the square of the hypotenuse without ever measuring an actual triangle, nor did we experience cause directly, where did the idea of cause come from?

Hume's answer is that "after the constant conjunction of two objects, heat and flame, for instance, weight and solidity, we determine by custom alone to expect the one from the appearance of the other."[4] Or, in Kant's lively language (though he claims, accurately, not to be able to write as "alluringly"[5] as Hume):

> [R]eason completely and fully deceives herself with this concept, falsely taking it for her own child, when it is really nothing but a bastard of the imagination, which, impregnated by experience, and having brought certain representations under the law of association, passes off the resulting subjective necessity (i.e. habit) for an objective necessity.[6]

And it is not just the concept of causation that Hume sweeps away. Kant argues that "metaphysics consists wholly of such concepts."[7] Philosophers for centuries had been speculating about the universe and things in it without, Kant thought, first adequately determining the status of these things and our relationship to them. This is why philosophy had been spinning its wheels for centuries without making any real progress the way other fields such as mathematics and the natural sciences did.

If Hume is right about causation, then science will have lost its firm foundation. If cause and effect is not necessary but simply a habit of the mind based on experience, then the connection of lightning and thunder is not a necessary one, though habit makes it feel necessary to us. We cannot be sure that lightning will cause thunder tomorrow. We cannot count on the repeatability of experiments. Newton's laws may accurately have described the motion of all objects in the universe until now, but they are not prescriptive, and we may have to change them tomorrow.

I begin Kant's solution to this problem with his definition of intuition (*Anschauung*). It will be important to hold on to this definition when we get to Schleiermacher's theory of religion (Chapter 4), because Kant and Schleiermacher both use this word in a specific sense that differs greatly from common English usage, and a misunderstanding here leads to great errors of interpretation. An intuition for Kant (and for Schleiermacher) is not some uncanny knowledge for which we can have no real evidence. "An intuition is a representation of the sort which would depend immediately on the presence of an object."[8] Right now you are having an intuition of the book you are holding. It is a representation in your mind, not the book itself (that would hurt). And it is completely normal, obvious, impossible to doubt. Kant's definition is almost the opposite of what we normally mean when we use the word "intuition" (there is another German word that comes much closer to that: *Ahnung*).

Note that your representation of the book comes to you a posteriori, through experience. There is no logical necessity that this book exist, or that you read it. You could not have shown a priori that this would be the case, as you can show a priori that $A^2 + B^2 = C^2$. But some parts of our experience are necessary, as obvious and normal and undeniable as the presence of the book in your hands. Kant argues that you can take a representation and remove almost all features of it (so, this book can be coverless, even wordless, and on and on), but you can never succeed in removing space or time. If you try to imagine a spaceless timeless book it ceases to exist for you. That any object you can perceive will exist in space and time is as obvious to you as the book you hold in your hands.

(And, to be clear, we are never talking about the book-in-itself for Kant, but always our representation of the book.) What accounts for these pure (as opposed to empirical) intuitions?

Kant's answer is as follows:

> There is therefore only one way possible for my intuition to precede the actuality of the object and occur as an a priori cognition, namely if it contains nothing else except the form of sensibility, which in me as subject precedes all actual impressions through which I am affected by objects. For I can know a priori that the objects of the senses can be intuited only in accordance with this form of sensibility.[9]

For Kant these forms of sensibility are space and time. We know with necessity that all external objects we experience will appear to us in space and time because space and time are features of our minds that organize and make experience possible in the first place.

Kant goes on to argue that, in addition to forms of intuition, our minds contain pure concepts of the understanding (he gives a table of 12 concepts), also a priori, under which we necessarily subsume representations caused by objects affecting our senses to sort and organize them. These concepts include such things as cause and substance. Kant titles the section of the first Critique in which he demonstrates these 12 fundamental concepts the "Transcendental Deduction of the Pure Concepts of the Understanding." Note Kant's use of the word "transcendental." "Transcendent" typically means something like: "Beyond or above the range of normal or physical human experience," and "transcendental" something like: "of or relating to the spiritual or nonphysical realm."[10] But again Kant means almost the opposite. It is precisely preoccupation with things surpassing human experience that has caused metaphysics to spin its wheels for so long. By "transcendental" Kant means an examination of what must be the case about human minds such that our experience of the world is possible. What are the conditions of possibility of our experience?

We do not experience objects in any simple way, as Hume seems to think. We are not blank slates. Rather, our experiences (what Kant calls phenomena) are a combination of the effect that things-in-themselves (Kant calls these noumena) have on us, and the way our sensibility and understanding shape these. We never experience things directly, but we always experience *as*—as appearing in space and time and ordered according to the concepts of the understanding.

This is what Kant calls his Copernican revolution in metaphysics, or "the turn to the subject." Metaphysics for Kant is not a matter of speculating about how and what the world is outside of us, it is a matter of deducing what our minds must be like such that we experience the world the way we do. This may at first glance seem to contradict how the world seems to be. Things like space and cause do seem to be out there, part of nature. But Kant argues that they are only features of nature so long as we define nature as "nothing in itself but a sum of appearances, hence not a thing in itself but merely a multitude of representations of the mind."[11] And if we allow him to make that move then he has the great advantage of having secured our knowledge and the reliability of science from Hume's challenge. If the concept of cause and effect is not merely a habit of our minds developed by our repeated experience of conjoined objects (which might not be conjoined tomorrow), if rather cause and effect is an a priori feature of our minds by which we necessarily organize experiences, then there is no possibility that tomorrow they will change. They are as secure as $A^2 + B^2 = C^2$. We will always necessarily organize our experience the same way.

The corollary of this view is that Kant draws a veil between subject and object—we will always experience the same way, but we will never experience or know anything about things-in-themselves. We do not even have privileged access to ourselves. We only know ourselves through representations of ourselves, as we experience ourselves, which is to say as appearing in time (and as bodies in space too), and as subsumed under the 12 pure concepts of the understanding, as well as other concepts. There may be things in the world that our sensory apparatus cannot pick up. They are simply off our radar screens. Of these human reason can tell us nothing. Our minds are not built to have knowledge of things that lie beyond our possible experience.

Experience, for Kant, unfolds roughly as follows:

> there are two stems of human cognition, which may perhaps arise from a common but to us unknown root, namely **sensibility** and **understanding**, through the first of which objects are given to us, but through the second of which they are thought.[12]

Sensibility gives us intuitions of objects, to which the understanding then applies concepts (i.e. makes judgments). Thinking for Kant just is the subsuming of appearances under concepts. As he famously writes, "Thoughts without content are empty, intuitions without concepts are blind."[13] Sensibility is receptive, passive; understanding is spontaneous, active.

The process actually is slightly more complicated than that. But that suffices to draw out the contrasts between Kant and Schleiermacher. The main themes to keep in mind are the following: for Kant experience is a combination of our minds' concepts, and the influence of things outside us. Because our experience is formed by these concepts, we have no direct access to things as they are independent of us. I refer to this as the Kantian veil. Further, these concepts are universal across humans. In important ways our minds are the same. Specifically, these pure concepts of the understanding are independent of language. In part because language plays a limited role in Kant's epistemology, knowledge has, in some ways, a nonsocial character.

Let us move from "the starry heavens above me" to "the moral law within me." According to Kant's moral theory, outlined in his second critique (*The Critique of Practical Reason*, 1788), our moral judgments are based not on the consequences of our actions, but on the principles on which we take ourselves to be acting. Kant calls these principles maxims. If someone does something for the right reason, we call that good, whether or not the action succeeds. Our ability, as rational beings, to do this, is the second thing that "fill[s] the mind with ever new and increasing admiration and awe" for Kant. In order to do something for the right reason we must be able freely to choose between actions. Kant argues that as rational beings humans are autonomous, that is, literally self-legislating. We have the ability to determine what actions are in accord with reason (not just in accord with our desires), and choose to do those actions because they are in accord with reason.

But if we experience ourselves under the same concepts as every other object in our world, especially the concept of cause, then it seems that we cannot know that we are free. Our actions are determined by the states of affairs that precede them. These states of affairs may be more complex than the action of one billiard ball on another that Hume takes as an example of cause and effect, but this is a difference of degree, not kind. Despite the fact that it feels like we are choosing freely and making moral determinations based on these choices, as phenomena we are like balls in a very complex billiards game. Kant acknowledges the problem, and calls it an antinomy. That is, there are good arguments that humans as rational beings are free, but equally good arguments that we are not. Reason cannot show that one set of arguments is better than the other. He struggles mightily through the rest of his philosophical life to show that humans are, in fact, free. But as we will see in Taylor's account of the reaction to Kant of the generation following him, these struggles were not persuasive, nor was the way he conceived of freedom in the first place. I turn now to this issue, and others related to his epistemology.

The Generation Following Kant

Charles Taylor, in his monumental book on Hegel, outlines the tasks confronting the generation of thinkers to which Hegel and Schleiermacher belonged. He groups these tasks into four classes of criticism of the radical Enlightenment and of Kant:

1 This generation "bitterly reproached the Enlightenment thinkers for having dissected man and hence distorted the true image of human life in objectifying nature."[14] Kant's split between sensibility and understanding seems to raise many of the same problems of dualism found in other philosophers.

2 They criticized the definition of freedom operative in Kant and other thinkers as "independence of the self-defining subject in relation to outside control."[15] For many of these thinkers freedom was not primarily a matter of independence from outside control; it had a deeper valence. It was the capacity for "self-realization which is the basic goal of men."[16] Kant found it hard to articulate how we can both be part of nature (phenomena) and independent of nature. Defining freedom as the ability to develop oneself as part of an unfolding natural process avoids this problem (though it may open up others). We will return to this idea of self-realization in Chapter 3; it is an important one for Schleiermacher.

3   They criticized the separation of humans from nature entailed in Enlightenment thought. "If I am not satisfied with an image of myself as a mind confronting internal and external nature, but must think of myself as life in which nature speaks through thought and will, if therefore I as a subject am one with my body, then I have to take account of the fact that my body is in interchange with the greater nature outside."[17] Avoiding the dualisms seen in criticisms 1 and 2 above allows one to frame the subject/object relationship differently.

4   The "communion with nature applies with the same force to communion with other men." This generation rejected the view (familiar to contemporary Americans through the economic theories of Adam Smith) that "society is made up of atomistic, morally self-sufficient subjects who enter into external relations with each other, seeking either advantage or the defence of individual rights."[18] While Kant's goal of a cosmopolitanism made up of autonomous (dignified) individuals has a lot of appeal, Kant's critical philosophy does not offer a robust way of describing the way that communities and individuals are always shaping each other. Schleiermacher's generation sought a way to conceive of a deeper bond that formed a community. Many took as a model of this community the ancient Greek *polis*.

Kant's emphasis on autonomy was appealing to these thinkers, but Kant shared with other Enlightenment figures the definition of freedom as freedom from external control. The chief of these external forces for Kant was desire. In Kant to be free comes close to meaning to be able to act in the face of one's desires. One acts out of respect for the rational law in spite of one's desires. Kant literally objectified nature, drew a veil between knowing subjects and known objects. Kant had difficulty articulating the importance to individuals of living in a culture or community with others.

It is worth keeping these criticisms in mind as we look at Schleiermacher's Dialectic and Philosophical Ethics. They explain in part some of the choices he makes, particularly in the assumptions he feels he must make as the starting points of working out his epistemology and his theory of history.

Schleiermacher's Dialectic

Having spent a fair amount of time sketching out Kant's epistemology, we have already done a good portion of the work necessary to understand Schleiermacher's epistemology. The work that fulfills roughly the same tasks in his body of works as the *Critique of Pure Reason* does in Kant's is Schleiermacher's *Lectures on Dialectic*.[19] Schleiermacher's Dialectic is a formal theory of knowledge (or science). Before launching into Schleiermacher's epistemology, I want to describe the way Schleiermacher organizes the various fields of knowledge.[20] This will help us keep track of the various discussions of Schleiermacher's intellectual output for the rest of the book, and help us see how he relates them to each other.

When it comes to the actual work of gaining knowledge, Schleiermacher argues that there are two basic "real" sciences, ethics and physics. Just as knowledge has an intellectual and an organic side (thinking is organizing representations stemming from stimuli affecting our senses), "[t]he sense of opposition [of ethics and physics] is inborn in the form of soul and body, the ideal and the real, reason and nature."[21]

Within the two basic sciences of physics and ethics, Schleiermacher makes further subdivisions. Each of the two basic sciences can be subdivided into speculative and empirical parts. Schleiermacher's Philosophical Ethics, as a theory of history and culture, fall under speculative ethics. His studies of what people have actually thought and done fall under empirical ethics. These fields include historical theology, Christian ethics, and, importantly, Christian Dogmatics. This is a key point to which we will return in Chapter 5 ("Mediating Theology").

To complete Schleiermacher's architectonic of knowledge (Figure 2.1), there are several "mixed sciences" which are both speculative and empirical. Critical disciplines provide a moral critique of history, so they examine empirically what people have thought and done, and judge this by standards arrived at speculatively. Political philosophy and philosophy of religion fall here. Technical disciplines make use of speculative principles to train leaders to accomplish specific (empirical) tasks. Pedagogy and practical theology fall here.[22]

Formal Theory of Knowledge (Science)	Dialectic			
The Sciences	Physics Science of Nature		Ethics Science of Reason/History	
Kinds of Knowledge	Speculative Physics	Empirical Physics	Speculative Ethics (e.g. Philosophical Ethics)	Empirical Ethics (e.g. Christian Dogmatics and Ethics) Historical Theology
Mixed Sciences			Critical (knowledge) Philosophical Theology	Technical (action) Practical Theology

FIGURE 2.1 *Schleiermacher's architectonic of knowledge*

With this architectonic of knowledge before us, we turn to what it means, for Schleiermacher, to know something in the first place. We turn to his epistemology. I want at the start to assert that there are ways in which Schleiermacher thinks we know less than Kant thinks we know, and ways in which Schleiermacher thinks we know more. But Schleiermacher is careful not to pierce the Kantian veil. He does not seek to get around or behind it to things-in-themselves. I will leave it to the reader at the end of this section to make a judgment about whether or not Schleiermacher's epistemology works as well as Kant's. But as we discuss the Dialectic I want to state Schleiermacher's unwillingness to pierce the Kantian veil as bluntly as possible. Like Kant, Schleiermacher holds that we never experience things-in-themselves.

Schleiermacher's Dialectic asks a related but different question than Kant's first Critique. Rather than "What are the conditions of the possibility of experience?" Schleiermacher asks "How do we move from thinking to knowing?" We can know something, according to Schleiermacher, when two things are the case. First, we must connect our thoughts properly (logic). Significant portions of the Dialectic concern logic. Second, we know something when our thoughts stand in the proper relationship to the objects we are thinking about, that is, when thinking and being are in accord. This is metaphysics. In this discussion I will have little to say about logic; I will have a fair amount to say about Schleiermacher's metaphysics.

Schleiermacher acknowledges that "Dialectic" has a bad connotation, and has become associated with sophistry. Kant writes of the term:

> As different as the significance of the employment of this designation of a science or art among the ancients may have been, one can still infer from their actual use of it that it was nothing other than the logic of illusion.[23]

For Kant, "dialectic" has been used in the past to refer to the kinds of speculation about things he thinks humans simply cannot know. Kant tries to alter the word's usage to refer to the critical task of reasoning about the limits of our knowledge (just as Kant tries to alter the usage of the word "transcendental").

But Schleiermacher wants to rehabilitate the word "dialectic" for at least two reasons. First is his claim that thinking becomes knowledge when it corresponds with being. Thus metaphysics cannot be avoided; we need to give some account of being. This is one significant departure from Kant. The term "Dialectic" predates Aristotle, for whom philosophy was not a discipline separate from ethics and physics (study of humans and study of nature). Schleiermacher will want to ground ethics and physics in a certain kind of metaphysical philosophy.

Second, the word "dialectic" etymologically means "the art of undertaking and leading conversation" (p. 119). This indicates for Schleiermacher the profoundly social nature of our experience and knowledge, and this is a second significant departure from Kant. Schleiermacher writes, "one does not undertake a conversation when one is completely of one mind" (p. 119). It is only in discussion with others that we begin to move toward confidence that we have in fact followed the rules of logic, and that our thinking does begin to be more and more in harmony with being.

As a kind of general principle Schleiermacher tries not to make binary contrasts, rather he tends to place things in relation to each other on a spectrum or scale. We will see this several times in his thought. Schleiermacher argues that "there is no thought in which both . . . the intellectual and the organic side are not together" (p. 148). This corresponds to Kant's distinction of two stems of human cognition: understanding and sensibility. Schleiermacher defines "organic" as "the effect of posited being outside us on our organs" (p. 161). For Schleiermacher the organic part of knowing is receptive or determined (things in the world impinge on us), the intellectual is active, spontaneous, lively. But Schleiermacher, who has less of a stark mind/body dualism than Kant, argues that, while both the intellectual and the organic are present, they are present more or less. When the organic aspect predominates, we call this perception. When the intellectual aspect predominates, we call this thinking in the narrow sense. When the organic and intellectual aspects are in balance, we call this intuition (p. 153). If the intellectual side is completely absent (the bottom end of the scale) we have not thinking but chaos. If the organic side is absent (the top end of the scale) we have "the thought of the highest being" (p. 152). But this is not a real thought, not something we can know, for reasons that will become clear below.

For Schleiermacher as for Kant, thinking just is the applying of concepts to representations. The act of doing this is judgment. So concepts function the same way in Schleiermacher's epistemology as they do in Kant's. But here again we see Schleiermacher's basic way of thinking, which is to place things on a spectrum and describe the bottom and top and of that spectrum. To think is to subsume under a concept. Concepts must be organized hierarchically to function as concepts. There is no "concept of an individual," concepts group things together (p. 172). That means that concepts are ranked in a hierarchy of less to more general. So we can judge that an object is the color "burgundy," but only because "burgundy" falls under a more general concept of "red." "Red" in turn falls under the more general concept of "color," and "color" in turn under a more general concept.

It is not possible to "think" at either the bottom or the top of the scale because to think is to subsume under concepts. Concepts always hover between lower (less universal) and higher (more universal) concepts, and so at the bottom and top ends of the hierarchy of concepts there is no concept under which to subsume. At the bottom is mere chaos, individuality not grouped together, receptive organic stimulation without intellect. Schleiermacher writes,

> Finally what comes out is the relatedness of each object with all others, that is the mere modifiability of the object. But this is nothing other than the inexhaustible manifold of judgments. This is the lowest point of concept. Because here judgments are infinite, so too there is no complete concept of an individual. (p. 172)

Nothing is subsumed under a concept, and so there is no thought.

At the top end of the scale thought again becomes impossible. If thinking is the placing representations under concepts, and concepts make distinctions because they fall under higher concepts, then at the top of the scale of concepts we must assume something more general than any concept.

> The highest would then be where the opposition of concept and object is suspended (*aufgehoben*). That would be the same that we regarded as the transcendental, the being in which the opposition of ideal and real is suspended. But this we cannot consider as knowledge. . . . It is a mere assumption (*Setzung*), that can only be compared to the totality of all combinations. (p. 172)

We cannot account for knowing without this assumption (p. 165), but we cannot think it or perceive it, "of an intuition thereof can there be absolutely no talk" (p. 164), because it is not a concept, it does not hover beneath something more general. "The universal identity of being remains for us completely behind the curtain" (p. 164).

This is the absolute or the transcendent for Schleiermacher. Whereas Kant shifted the meaning of the word "transcendental" to refer to a critique of the mind's powers and limits, Schleiermacher retains the more common usage of the term to refer to things beyond the human mind. But like Kant, Schleiermacher argues that we cannot know the transcendental. As we will see in Chapters 4 and 5, Christians have a language for talking about this absolute, but, as he points out in the *Dialectic*, this falls in the realm not of knowledge but in the realm of "belief" (p. 164). We posit but do not know the absolute, the transcendent. Schleiermacher offers no way to get behind the curtain.[24]

One of the most significant departures of Schleiermacher's epistemology from Kant's is that, for Schleiermacher, concepts depend on language. Kant's 12 pure concepts of the understanding are innate, and universal across humans. Additional concepts for Kant seem to be acquired and related to language in some way, though Kant gives no good account of this. Schleiermacher writes,

> In the typical doctrine of innate concepts, in particular in the Leibnizian philosophy, a contrast is made between the innate and the acquired concepts, which contrast we absolutely cannot make. (p. 192)

Where then do concepts come from? "Language is on the whole the natural production of concepts" (p. 275). "One could say, that for the most part each of the general concepts that he has he did not produce by himself, but took from tradition" (p. 151).

I wrote above that Schleiermacher's epistemology differs from Kant's in two significant ways. Both involve his use of the word "dialectic." First, there is a different relationship of our thinking to the objects we think about than we find in Kant. For Schleiermacher as we move from thinking to knowing our thinking becomes more and more in accord with being. For Kant we never move closer to knowing being. We move from thinking to knowing when we adequately critique our use of concepts. The second difference is the communal nature of knowledge in Schleiermacher. Kant tends to speak of the experience of an individual, assuming that this will work the same way for all humans. Schleiermacher assumes that the process of human experience and knowledge is not individual but social. Both these differences have their origin in the linguistic roots of concepts for Schleiermacher.

When Schleiermacher asks, "How do we move from thinking to knowing?" he answers that we do so when we think logically, and when our thinking is in accord with being. That means for Schleiermacher that we cannot avoid metaphysics—we need to know something about being to know when our thinking is in accord with it.[25] This requirement leads Schleiermacher to posit several things about being:

All being must be taken up in the entire system of concepts, it must relate to itself in itself as higher and lower, when there is no absolute highest and absolute lowest. That is, this is the essence of the concept, that each, be it whichever it may be, has a higher over it, and must contain a lower in it. Should being correspond to that, so must such an opposition be in it [being]. That is: what is individualized in being may not be posited as an absolute independent, rather it is a source of other being that in a subordinate way is independent, and stands under a higher [being] through which its independence is limited [*begrenzt*]. (p. 198)

In order for us to know, being itself must be structured hierarchically, in a way to which the structure of thinking corresponds. Knowing would require that being be arranged hierarchically, with each individual being dependent on a being above it, and the source of beings below it. At the bottom end of the hierarchy of being are chaotic individual things, at the top end absolute being (which Christians call God). But again, it is important to stress that our hierarchy of concepts runs out at the top and the bottom of the hierarchy and so the top and bottom cannot be thought, so for Schleiermacher we must assume a top and bottom of the hierarchy of being, but we can never think or know them at all. This is more about being than Kant is willing to posit (though Kant does argue in his third Critique that our experience of beauty depends on certain hints about the structure of nature corresponding to the structure of our minds).

It might seem that, in supposing that being is structured in this way, Schleiermacher is violating the strict Kantian limits of what we can know. But Schleiermacher does not claim that we ever know being completely, ever get the hierarchy of being exactly right. The move from thinking to knowing is not binary but again lies on a spectrum. Through the communal process of subsuming intuitions under concepts we get ever closer to an adequate idea of being. The process is progressively corrective, but never complete.

Second, concepts for Schleiermacher depend on language. And so thinking and knowing must be communal, not just because we make corrective progress by thinking together, but because the very tools of thinking are given to us by our community. You are born into a language. And as we will see in Chapter 3 (Hermeneutics), the way you use language affects the language, and therefore the concepts available to others in your community. To think is to subsume under concepts, and concepts are given to us in language. Schleiermacher writes, "the identity of thought . . . is determined through the identity of language. This makes the natural border" (p. 158).

Kant agrees that some concepts may be given to us empirically (he does not specifically mention through the learning of a language, but this would have to fall here). But this cannot be the case for the 12 pure a priori concepts, because that would call their necessity and unchangeability into question.

> It is therefore clear that only a transcendental and never an empirical deduction of them [pure concepts] can be given, and that in regard to pure *a priori* concepts empirical deductions are nothing but idle attempts, which can occupy only those who have not grasped the entirely distinctive nature of these cognitions.[26]

This is a price Schleiermacher is willing to pay, in part because knowledge is a process and not an event for him. This approach is only possible in a community that gives us the concepts in the first place, and gives us interlocutors with whom we argue, correct, discuss, and become more accurate in the correlation of concepts and being. The sign of knowledge will be more widespread agreement. But, such agreement is only a sign, not a guarantee. And the limit of agreement is the limit of any given language. Schleiermacher can even write, in the 1811 *Dialectics*, of "national reason."[27]

I think Kant would find this unacceptable for two reasons. The first thing Kant would find unacceptable is that in talking about the way being must be structured, Schleiermacher says more about being than Kant thinks is allowed. Schleiermacher talks about our representations of the world, but also of the way the world itself must be structured for knowing to occur. (Though note carefully the grammar of Schleiermacher's quote above: Schleiermacher phrases his claim not in terms of what being is like, but in terms of what being must be like if we are to account for the experience of knowing.) In this sense Schleiermacher claims to know more than Kant. Second, for Kant, our representations of the world will necessarily be ordered in certain ways. He has secured our knowledge against Humean skepticism. But knowledge for Schleiermacher is something toward which we, in a community of inquirers, make progress. In staying within the limits of possible human experience and knowledge, Schleiermacher has found it necessary to sacrifice the a priori necessary (and therefore completely confident) aspect of science that Kant set out to save. To return to our example of causation, Kant wants to secure causal relations with necessity. And he can do this because cause is purely an a priori necessary feature of our minds. Schleiermacher agrees that cause is a mental concept. But the word "cause" may carry slightly different connotations in different languages, and so be a slightly different concept. Furthermore, knowledge rests on the positing of cause also as a feature of nature (beings are the source of beings lower than them on the hierarchy of being). As humans experience and experiment more and more over time we learn to line up our conceptual cause with the cause of being better and better, that is, we get closer to knowledge. But the process is never complete. This is a big sacrifice, though one perhaps more in line with the contemporary philosophy of science and practice of scientists (for whom in the twentieth century, Newton's laws, for example, have been subsumed under apparently more complete and accurate laws of physics). In this sense that Schleiermacher claims to know less than Kant.[28]

Ethics

Almost all of Schleiermacher's activities fall under the category he labels "ethics." That is to say, while he kept abreast of developments in what English speakers call the natural sciences (what he calls physics), he himself is not a natural scientist. Schleiermacher defines ethics far more broadly than we typically do today. It is not merely a theory of how humans determine what they should do and why, though that is a part of ethics.[29] "Ethics, as the depiction of the way in which reason and nature coexist, is the science of history."[30] In our current usage, it is a theory of culture as well as of history.

As we have seen, Schleiermacher does not make absolute distinctions, but places things on a spectrum. While nature is material, it always contains or is shaped by at least a minimum of reason.

Likewise reason is not independent of nature but is embodied. In "everything which does occur there is reasonable nature and natural or organic reason."[31] Humans, physical beings possessing reason, are the organ of reason, the means by which reason works on nature.

> Ethics can only depict the possibility of penetrating and forming nature to an ever-increasing degree, of spreading as broadly as possible the unification of reason and nature, taking as its starting-point the human organism, which is a part of general nature in which, however, a unification with reason is already given.[32]

Ethics as a field encompasses all human activity, most particularly the activity (according to Schleiermacher) that furthers the interpenetration of reason and the material world. And here Schleiermacher makes a very important assertion. There is a point to human history; it has a trajectory. History is teleological. History is a process of the increasing unification of reason with nature, through the organ of human beings, natural animals possessed of reason. Nature, the material world, starts with a minimum (but never null) of reason. It is the raw material. "The ethical process is thus to be extended in every direction until the raw material dwindles to a minimum."[33] Each particular field of human endeavor plays a role in a larger scheme of the interpenetration of nature and reason.

Schleiermacher provides an overview of the various arenas of human life in the *Ethics*, an overview we can capture in a second heuristically useful chart (Figure 2.2). Ethics, as the study of human activity, is broken down into four subfields. These are the categories that correspond most naturally to different parts of our human efforts to think and to act, and so these categories are useful in tracking the various spheres in which Schleiermacher himself was active.

Schleiermacher achieves these four categories by arguing (and we can see why by referring back to his Dialectic), that a human life is both passive and active. It "is merely an interaction and sequence of taking-things-into-oneself and taking-things-out-of-oneself-and-putting-them-down."[34] Reason has a cognitive side, where we represent to ourselves what is happening, and an organizing side, where we make things happen, we change and shape the world.

Furthermore, reason is posited in nature both as a "relative being-posited-in-one's-own-right and a being posited-in-community."[35] Humans think (symbolizing function) and act (organizing function) sometimes alone and sometimes with others. If we form a table by crossing these two conceptual distinctions (never fully distinguished in fact), we end up with four boxes (Figure 2.2). Each box has a particular sphere of human activity, and with each is associated a particular institution or institutions in which those activities are set.

The communal organizing box contains the economic and political aspects of our lives. The institution created to pursue these is the state. The individual organizing box contains the aspects of our life having to do with social relations and hospitality. Schleiermacher does not name an institution here but one can easily imagine that these aspects are nourished in the salons of his Berlin youth.

The communal symbolizing box contains our efforts at knowledge and science. The institutions dedicated to these pursuits are schools, universities, and academies. The individual symbolizing activities are art and religion. The institution for these activities is the church. As a preacher, a university professor, an activist, a husband and father, and a socially gifted talker, Schleiermacher is

	Organizing	Symbolizing
Communal	economics, politics (the state)	knowledge, science (schools, universities, academies)
Individual	social relations, hospitality (salons?)	art, religion (the church)

FIGURE 2.2 *Schema of human activity.* "Salons" *is followed by a question mark because there is no one institution dedicated to social relations. Salons are an appropriate place for this activity, but they are not formal institutions nor are they the only place this activity occurs.*

active in most of these "boxes." In the following chapters on his Hermeneutics, his theory of religion, his theology, and his political activity, it will be helpful to refer back to this chart (Figure 2.2), so we can keep clear on the ways in which Schleiermacher conceived of his various activities as being distinct yet related.

In this chapter I have set out some of Schleiermacher's basic intellectual commitments and how he divides the various fields of human activity and thought by stating some of the basic arguments in his lectures on Dialectic and Philosophical Ethics. From the Dialectic the key points are as follows: thinking for Schleiermacher, as for Kant, is the subsuming of intuitions under concepts. For Schleiermacher these concepts are linguistic, and they are organized hierarchically, ranked by level of generality. There is no break between the pure basic concepts of the understanding and other concepts. Kant would find this unacceptable, because for him some concepts (like cause) must be innate, not derived from language or experience or tradition, lest their absolute necessity and unchangeability be called into question. In this sense Schleiermacher thinks we can know less than Kant thinks we can.

At the top and bottom of this scale of concepts we reach the limits of human thinking, and therefore of knowledge. Because every concept hovers beneath a higher one we must posit an absolute at the top of the scale, a unity of thinking and being. This positing has an analogue in Kant, but as a feature of his *Critique of Practical Reason*, not his epistemology.

Schleiermacher begins his epistemology with a slightly different question than Kant. Rather than asking "What are the conditions of the possibility of experience?" Schleiermacher asks "How do we move from thinking to knowing?" To know for both Kant and Schleiermacher means that our thinking is in harmony with being. But Kant means by this only the being of appearances—beyond that, to things-in-themselves, we cannot go. Schleiermacher thinks that knowing is a matter of aligning thinking with being as it really is. He does not think we ever achieve this completely, but the process is progressive and communal. In this sense, though I argue Schleiermacher does not pierce the Kantian veil, Schleiermacher does think we work toward more knowledge than Kant thinks we can have. He does not pierce the veil but moves very close to it. Perhaps it is fair to say that, compared to Kant's epistemology,

Schleiermacher's epistemology weakens the certainty of our knowledge but widens its scope.[36]

Schleiermacher's Ethics begins with the assertion that history is the process of reason penetrating nature ever more. Humans are the organ of this progressive process. This is quite an assumption, though again we find something analogous in Kant when he distinguishes natural description from natural history (a teleological framework imposed by humans), and argues that humans must impose such a teleological account to make sense of the data they study.[37] Or again Kant argues in this *Critique of the Power of Judgment* that the experience of beauty stems from the sense we get that nature is in fact constituted in such a way that it corresponds to human cognition, that nature is providential, not just arbitrary. But these assertions have a different status in Kant, coming as regulative principles that are corollaries of other projects, not as assumptions at the start of a body of inquiry.

Returning to the challenges facing the thinkers following Kant as outlined by Charles Taylor, we can see why Schleiermacher felt the need to make these assertions. First, for Schleiermacher humans do not stand over-against an objectified nature, rather they play a critical role in the unfolding of the progress of nature toward reason. In a sense, when Kant writes, "there are two stems of human cognition, which may perhaps arise from a common but to us unknown root, namely **sensibility** and **understanding**, through the first of which objects are given to us, but through the second of which they are thought," Schleiermacher, as do others in his generation, need to say something about this common but unknown root. For Schleiermacher it is the unfolding process of reason penetrating nature. Second, humans are part of the unfolding of nature, so freedom does not have to be defined as autonomy from external natural influences. Humans, as the organ in the ethical process of a history moving toward the telos of reason penetrating matter, work in accord with nature when they pursue their passions and plans. Third, the subject/object split is not as stark as in Kant, nor is the mind/body dualism. Humans are the intersection of reason and nature, and our minds are shaped by historical processes, not constituted by innate concepts independent of nature. Finally, Schleiermacher has a way of accounting for the relationship of humans to their communities at a very deep and constitutive level. As fundamentally linguistic beings humans, at the very deepest level of how they think and experience, are created by the language they hold in common with their community. And their actions and articulations in turn shape that community and their fellow members. It is to this last aspect of Schleiermacher's thought, the linguistic nature of humans and how we relate to each other, in effect, in a sea of language, that we turn in more detail in the next chapter, Hermeneutics.

CHAPTER THREE

Hermeneutics

In the previous chapter we saw how important language is for Schleiermacher's account of how we experience, think, and know the world. While his epistemology works in some ways similarly to Kant's, the concepts under which appearances are subsumed for Schleiermacher are always linguistic. This means that humans are fundamentally, not contingently, linguistic beings.[1] In this Schleiermacher agrees with others of his generation, perhaps most notably Wilhelm von Humboldt and Johann Gottfried Herder. It is the use Schleiermacher makes of this insight that leads many in the secondary literature to refer to him as the "father of hermeneutics" (hermeneutics is the art or science of interpretation). That claim may be exaggerated in a way that it is not when he is called the "father of modern theology," but we will see below the extent to which it is justifiable.

In this chapter I will describe the basic features of Schleiermacher's Hermeneutics. I will then point out some of the criticisms of his Hermeneutics, in particular the complaint that he overly "psychologizes" the process of interpretation, requiring an imaginative leap into the mind of the author or speaker being interpreted, and the argument, most prominently associated with Hans-Georg Gadamer, that Schleiermacher does not account for the dynamic properties of language itself. Finally I will be in a position to describe more fully Schleiermacher's theory of human nature, which we can usefully get at by placing it into the category of what

Isaiah Berlin and Charles Taylor would call an "expressivist" self.[2] Having done this we will have laid the groundwork for an accurate understanding of Schleiermacher's theory of religion (Chapter 4), some central points of his theology (Chapter 5), and his political contributions (Chapter 6).

The Basics

There are many forerunners to Schleiermacher's theory of Hermeneutics. Hermeneutics had traditionally been understood as a technical field offering guidelines and tools for the interpretation of problematic ancient texts. Of primary concern of course had been biblical texts, but also "classics" in Greek and Latin. If Schleiermacher has any claim to being a seminal figure in this field it is because of his conviction that every linguistic interaction, not just with ancient and fragmentary texts but also everyday conversations, requires interpretation and so falls under the discipline of Hermeneutics.[3]

We saw in Chapter 2 the close connection for Schleiermacher of thought and language. One could almost say that thought is the inside of language, language the outside of thought for him.[4] If a speech act[5] is an interior thought made public, the goal of interpretation is to work back from the public expression to the thought in the speaker's mind. Literal interpretation, for Schleiermacher, means something like accurately getting to what the speaker thought he or she was saying to his or her intended audience.[6]

Schleiermacher's Hermeneutics is divided into two basic parts, the grammatical and the technical. The grammatical part considers speech acts (including written texts) as a product of language; the technical part considers speech acts as the product of an individual.

Proper grammatical interpretation requires that the interpreter knows as much as possible about the language or dialect that the author/speaker was using and shared with his or her audience at the time he or she used it. One must be aware of the speaker's historical context, education, occupation, and so on. One must know the genre being used by the speaker or writer, and what the state of that genre was at the time of the speech act.[7] The grammatical task can obviously never be completed; it is an ongoing process. It may be simpler if one is having a conversation with a contemporary who shares a mother tongue but even then the task is not to be taken for granted, and the more one can learn about genre, context, history, and so on the better one can understand one's interlocutor.

The technical part of Hermeneutics considers speech acts as products of a particular individual. In part every speaker or writer reproduces standard meanings (else language would be incomprehensible), but at the same time every author or speaker produces something new (else there is not much point in producing the speech act). What is new in the speech act is an expression of the speaker's personality. The newness of a speech act falls on a continuum. Something like a shopping list or business ledger may not express much individuality, whereas certain forms of literature or some genres of speech may be highly original and bear a clear stamp of a single person's personality. Style is not a superficial matter of ornamentation, rather it is a central part of interpretation. Each speaker has his or her own style because each speaker combines the available language and with his or her individuality in every act of speech or writing.[8]

Schleiermacher classifies Hermeneutics as an art because, though it follows rules, there are no rules to guide the interpreter in the application of those rules.[9] Neither grammatical nor technical interpretation can succeed without the other. We must then go back and forth, applying each in turn, but it is not possible to stipulate in advance when one approach or the other must be applied.

The hermeneutical task is never complete.[10] We have already noted that the grammatical task is unending. One never has complete knowledge of a language, including one's mother tongue. On the technical side, one has no direct access to another's mind (despite how some people have read Schleiermacher—about which, more below). And so Schleiermacher argues that there is a hermeneutical circle. This circle is actually a series of circles, but the main idea is that good interpretation requires continued engagement (I sometimes tell my students struggling with difficult texts that there is no reading, only rereading). You can only grasp a text as a whole by understanding individual passages. But accurate interpretation of individual passages requires that one has read through the text as a whole. You can better interpret a text if you see its place in an author's corpus, but of course you can only master a corpus of readings one text at a time. You can only understand the significance of the body of work of an author by placing it in context with the work of the author's contemporaries. But again, you can only take on one author at a time. The better you get to know someone the better you can interpret the nuances of word choice, tone, inflection, and so on. But you can only get to know someone one interaction (through text, voice, or other media) at a time. You can only see what the standard use of language (the grammatical task) is at a given time by reading one author at a time and making comparisons to see what is distinctive about this author's language use (the technical task). But the circle is by no means a vicious one. A well-formed hermeneutical circle makes ever more progress toward better and better interpretation.

Issues in Schleiermacher's Hermeneutics

There have been at least two significant criticisms of Schleiermacher's Hermeneutics. I raise them not just to make readers aware of them, and I have no stake in raising them in order to show that Schleiermacher, in the end, is correct about everything. Rather, working through these criticisms will lead to a more nuanced understanding of Schleiermacher's Hermeneutics. First, Schleiermacher has been accused of "overpsychologizing," that is, requiring a leap by the interpreter into the mind of the speaker. This has been perhaps the most consistent criticism made of him, and is related to other criticisms made of his philosophy (as we saw in Chapter 2), his theory of religion (as we will see in Chapter 4), and his theology (as we will see in Chapter 5). Second, Schleiermacher has been criticized for locating the creativity and dynamism of language exclusively in the speaker or writer, and making language itself a rather dead tool. Language, it is argued, has its own instabilities and creative drives apart from the personalities of its users. I will have a lot to say about this first criticism, a little about the second.

The story most often told about Schleiermacher's Hermeneutics is that he puts too much stock into getting into the author's or speaker's mind. This is the view presented in an older book that still often serves as a standard introduction to Hermeneutics in English, Richard E. Palmer's *Hermeneutics: Interpretation Theory in Schleiermacher, Dilthey, Heidegger, and Gadamer*.[11] This is one line of criticism in Hans-Georg Gadamer's *Truth and Method*, and one can see it repeated many places, for example, in a 1979 article by Cornel West.[12]

The source of this reading (misreading, I claim) lies in part in Schleiermacher's texts themselves. Schleiermacher never prepared a version of the *Hermeneutics* for publication. Until the publication of Manfred Frank's edition in 1977, the best version available was put together by Friedrich Lücke from Schleiermacher's lecture notes and from notes taken by students at those lectures. It was published in 1838. As in other versions of the *Hermeneutics*, the second part of this text takes up technical interpretation. Technical interpretation, as I described above, is the part of the hermeneutical task that focuses on the speech act as the product of a specific individual, the imprint of the speaker's personality on the language. As part of this section, in the 1838 version, Schleiermacher introduces a subsection on psychological interpretation. This has been taken by many to indicate that, while the earlier Schleiermacher kept his focus on language and stressed the grammatical side of interpretation, the late Schleiermacher moved toward emphasizing psychology, getting inside the author's head, to a much greater extent.[13]

Schleiermacher says of technical interpretation, "the unity of the work, the theme, is here regarded as the principle which moves the writer, and the basic characteristics of the composition as his individual nature which reveals itself in that moment."[14] He offers two methods for this technical task, the divinatory method "in which one, *so to speak*, transforms oneself into the other person and tries to understand the individual element directly," and the comparative method, which "posits the person to be understood as something universal and then finds the individual aspect by comparison with other things included under the same universal."[15]

It is not hard to see how talk of divination, and of transforming oneself into another person, would set off alarms for those who think that Schleiermacher has a tendency to jump out of the bounds of normal human cognition and "know" things that Enlightenment thinkers such as Kant had shown to be unknowable. Palmer argues, for example, that the divinatory method allows one to make "somehow, a kind of leap into the hermeneutical circle," by which "one goes out of himself and transforms himself into the author so that he can grasp in full immediacy the latter's mental process."[16] Bruce Marshall writes, divination is "concerned to grasp in an immediate, intuitive, nonconceptualizable way the unique individuality and thoughts of an author."[17]

But there are several reasons why I think this accusation of "overpsychologizing," of some kind of unmediated leap into the mind of another, is not the best reading of Schleiermacher. First, throughout the *Hermeneutics*, Schleiermacher constantly stresses the need to oscillate between the grammatical and technical tasks. This does not diminish over time. There is not an unbalanced tilt toward the technical or psychological in the later Schleiermacher. In fact, one of the texts that had traditionally been thought to be one of the latest, consisting of parallels between grammatical and technical interpretation, has been shown to be one of the earliest. Manfred Frank followed Hermann Patsch's suggested date of 1826–27 for this fragment. But Wolfgang Virmond has argued convincingly, based on the size, type, and watermark of the paper used, that the fragment is from 1805. Schleiermacher relied on this manuscript fragment in preparing his last set of lectures on Hermeneutics, the 1832/33 lectures.[18] So there seems to be more consistency between the early and the late Schleiermacher on the balance of grammatical and technical interpretation than had been thought.

Second, Schleiermacher insists that the divinatory method is possible only because of "the fact that everyone carries a minimum of everyone else within himself, and divination is consequently excited by comparison with oneself."[19] In other words the divinatory method always works together with the comparative, and together they comprise the technical, which always works together with the grammatical. Scholars who criticize Schleiermacher for wanting to get into other people's heads often omit the clause "so to speak" when discussing Schleiermacher's claim that in the divinatory method "one, so to speak, transforms oneself into the other person and tries to understand the individual element directly."[20] The divinatory is not a mystical leap but the principle that if you know yourself to some extent then you already know at least a little bit about others. Knowledge of yourself is the basis on which you can begin to make judgments about the motivations or goals of someone else (just as broad knowledge of others is the basis for the comparative method of beginning to make these same judgments about a speaker).

Why then does Schleiermacher add a section titled "Psychology"? Schleiermacher argues that we can distinguish two parts of technical interpretation (the task of understanding a speech act as the product of an individual). First, one's personality influences one's speech as an "indeterminate, fluid train of thoughts" (the way one thinks in general). Second, personality influences "the completed structure of thoughts" in this speech act (why one decides to speak this time, and in this way in this text).[21] I have certain dispositions that will be expressed in a speech. I also have specific intentions in most particular speech acts. There is "a constant quantity, a specific relation of every point to the proposed goal in comparison with every preceding point."[22] I will make particular rhetorical decisions. These moments complement each other; both belong to technical interpretation. Rather than reading Schleiermacher as moving more and more toward a theory that we can jump into other people's minds, I think the addition of a "psychological" section in later lectures is move toward an added distinction and element of nuance within technical interpretation.

The second criticism of Schleiermacher's Hermeneutics, also articulated by Gadamer, may have more merit. For Gadamer, Schleiermacher's Hermeneutics has to do with the tension between identical convention and individual production. The former stabilizes or fixes the meaning of language through repetition (what Schleiermacher calls "schematization").[23] Gadamer thinks this move on Schleiermacher's part is justified by his attempt to move away from theories of inspiration or of Platonic forms to account for meaning in language. The latter accounts for shifts in language, alterations of the schemas. Language is dynamic, Gadamer claims of Schleiermacher's theory, because of the creative force of individuals' novel uses of language.

Gadamer holds this to be an impoverished view of language. He claims that language makes itself vital, apart from the personalities of individual speakers. Speech is filled out with particularities and arbitrary factors that stem from language itself.[24] Here Gadamer does not claim that Schleiermacher emphasizes technical interpretation at the expense of grammatical interpretation. But Schleiermacher does emphasize technical interpretation in creative shifts in language at the expense of the creative properties inherent in language itself.

Paul Ricoeur, responding to Gadamer, has pointed out that Schleiermacher can account for some aspects of instability or change within language itself. For Schleiermacher, change can occur through polysemy (the existence of many possible meanings in a word or phrase). Ricoeur writes,

> It is worth noting that Schleiermacher placed this problem in grammatical hermeneutics and not in technical or psychological hermeneutics. This represents, precisely, an indeterminacy in language and one which is part of the common legacy; it is indeed language itself which displays this plural unity.[25]

But if it is the case that Gadamer has overstated the lack of dynamics in language itself in Schleiermacher, it is also certainly the case that, for better or worse, we find very little in Schleiermacher's Hermeneutics resembling a full discussion of deferred signification or presence complicated by nonpresence in language, the way we do in the works of deconstructionists and poststructuralists. Nor do we see a discussion in Schleiermacher of the possibility that the definitive interpretation of a text lies not in the intention of the writer, but in the text itself, or in the reader, or in some space "in front of" the text or between the text and the reader.

The Expressivist Self

Kant famously asks, "What can I know?" "What should I do?" "What may I hope?"[26] These fundamental questions about the meaning of human life rise in Kant's time with great force because many of the traditional answers to them no longer seemed very convincing. In the ancient and medieval worlds in Europe meaning was derived from finding one's proper place in a meaning-filled cosmos. But the underpinnings of these traditional answers had been called into question and could no longer be taken for granted, beginning with the assault of the late medieval nominalists on the existence of forms, and therefore of a worldview in which we dwell in a form-soaked cosmos. Traditional answers were further challenged by the Enlightenment attacks on epistemologies that accepted any easy sense of the authority of Scripture and tradition. And while the Enlightenment began with a very high opinion of human reason, it culminated in the careful circumscribing of the power of human reason to know the kinds of metaphysical truths we would have to know to locate meaning in the world outside us. One of the markers of modernity is precisely this shift from meaning as a seeming alignment with the cosmos to meaning being a task left up to humans themselves to create.

Kant's answers to these questions rest finally on his view that humans are essentially rational. But we saw in Chapter 2 that this view of reason, of humans as rational and autonomous, led to unbearable consequences for the generation immediately impacted by Kant. How can we know we are free? What is the relationship of subject and object, human and nature? What is the connection between humans such that we are fundamentally communal beings?

Charles Taylor has described one important set of attempts to work through these problems under the rubric of "expressivism." It is important to note that expressivism is not just one more among many theories of the self (or, in theological terms, theological anthropologies). Isaiah Berlin, to whom Taylor acknowledges his debts in articulating this theory, has written that expressivism is

> the largest recent movement to transform the lives and the thought of the Western world. It seems to me to be the greatest single shift in the consciousness of the West that has occurred, and all the other shifts which have occurred in the course of the nineteenth and twentieth centuries appear to me in comparison less important, and at any rate deeply influenced by it.[27]

In other words, though philosophers and political theorists often attribute modern and contemporary ideas of the self to Kant (the focus on autonomy and human dignity that underpin the notion of universal human rights), it is in fact the thinkers working with as well as reacting to Kant who have constructed what I believe is the default modern anthropology. (By anthropology I mean not the academic discipline but a theory about what it means to be fully human. My conviction, which I cannot work out here, is that most of us have an expressivist anthropology, whether we articulate it theoretically or simply assume it in prereflective ways.)

Taylor himself is not particularly interested in reading Schleiermacher, nor does he have any particular facility at interpreting him when he does. For Taylor the paradigmatic expressivists are Herder, Humboldt, and Hegel. I think, however, that Schleiermacher belongs on this list as one of the most influential creators and promulgators of the expressivist anthropology.[28] Given our work on Schleiermacher's Dialectic and the linguistic nature of concepts, on his Ethics, and on his Hermeneutics, we are in a great position to see why this is.

But what is expressivism? As Brent Sockness points out, expressivists return meaning to life that had been apparently sealed off by the radical Enlightenment and by Kant. Like the ancients they argue that "life is the realization of purpose."[29] But meaning now is located not in the cosmos, but in the individual. Schleiermacher writes that he has a deep appreciation of the "discovery of universal reason." And yet he has learned that there is something "still higher" than universal reason: "the unique nature which freedom chooses for herself in each individual." He continues:

> It became clear to me that each person should represent humanity in his or her own way, with a particular mixture of its elements, so that humanity reveals itself in each way and all becomes realized in the fullness of space and time.[30]

What it is to be human means to express or bring out our own subjectivity, or some state of our subjectivity.[31]

But one does not simply bring out into public view something preformed and finished. Sockness writes,

> [I]n my mind the most original and subtle feature of the expressivist theory, is the fact that on this conception of human nature the actualization and clarification of purposes go hand in hand. Taylor puts it this way: "If we think of our life as realizing an essence or form, this means not just the embodying of this form in reality, it also means defining in a determinate way what this form is. And this shows in another way the important difference between the expressivist model and the Aristotelian tradition: for the former the idea which a man realizes is not wholly determined beforehand; it is only made fully determinate in being fulfilled."[32]

What it means to be fully human on this model is to express, to bring out, what we essentially are. And it is only in the bringing out that this subjectivity is defined and formed in a determinate way. Goethe captures the basic idea nicely when a character in his novel *Wilhelm Meister's Apprenticeship* says:

> Everyone holds his fortune in his own hands, like the sculptor the raw material he will fashion into a figure. But it's the same with that type of artistic activity as with all others. Only the ability to do it, only the capability, is inborn in us, it must be learned and attentively cultivated.[33]

For Schleiermacher as for the other expressivists we have a moral duty, in religious terms a calling, to express our individuality. If we are denied this possibility, or do not take it upon ourselves to fulfill it, then we are not fully human, not fully playing our intended place in the ethical unfolding of history. This has a negative effect on others as well as on ourselves. As we saw in the *Hermeneutics* and the *Dialectic*, the language available to others as they work out their self-expression is in part constituted by the expressions of others in their community. If we fail to express ourselves and to imprint our personalities on the common language, we impoverish the resources available to others. We can only develop our individuality in community with, in comparison and contrast to, others around us. Schleiermacher writes,

> [E]ach should grant to the other freedom to go where the spirit drives him or her, and be helpful only where the other feels a lack not attributing to the other his or her own thoughts. In this way each would find in the other life and nourishment, and that which each could become, he or she would become fully.[34]

We can see why language, for Schleiermacher and his compatriots, is not accidentally or contingently human, but essentially human. Art becomes the paradigmatic human activity (especially poetry). This is the moment when art shifts from being a sophisticated craft, from being an imitation of nature, to being an expression of genius, and artists begin to take on the highly valued, almost priestly function that they still hold in the modern world. Artists see things the rest of us cannot, but artists can mediate this vision to us.

We can also see why I claimed, above, that expressivism becomes the "default" anthropology of the modern West. While it is based on a kind of freedom, as is Kant's, there is an important difference. For Kant freedom is freedom to be rational, to follow the moral law (to be autonomous, "self-legislating"). One can be free in this sense even if one is unjustly imprisoned, or sick, or in too much pain to act using one's full faculties. Freedom for Kant does not necessarily require that one be able to be a historical agent, to act in history, to express and impress one's individuality on the community and world outside oneself. One can still be autonomous, that is, act in accord with duty, and have dignity. But I think most of us are outraged by unjust imprisonment, by torture, most of us feel that pain is an obstacle to full humanity, precisely because we hold some kind of expressivist anthropology, articulated or not. Pain, wrongful imprisonment, are not just wrong or unfair. They are dehumanizing. They block the ability to be an agent, which is what it means for us to be fully human.[35]

Looking to previous chapters, we can see that language overlaps with reason, for Schleiermacher. And this reason overlaps substantially with the reason of others, though it is not universally the same the way Kant would have it. Each of us, because we use language slightly differently, is essentially individual, not iterations of a universal reason. This is entailed by his Dialectic. Each of us then has an obligation to develop ourselves, to express ourselves. If we do not we impoverish others. This is entailed by the Hermeneutics. Furthermore, each of us plays a unique role in the process of history, the ethical process of reason penetrating material ever more. No one else can fill our role for us. This is entailed by the Ethics.

Looking to the issues left behind by Kant, we can see how the theory of expressivism tries to overcome them. We are not separated from nature as subject to object. We are part of a natural process, an ethical unfolding. Our freedom is not the freedom to act in spite of natural causes or personal desires. Our freedom is the freedom to express and develop our natural individuality. And we are not separated from other humans atomistically, forming communities only through contracts. The community precedes the individual, as language precedes our thought and experience. We are given ourselves by our community, and in expressing and developing ourselves we shape and make that community possible.

Looking forward we will see how this expressivism informs Schleiermacher's theory of religion (Chapter 4), some of his most important theological doctrines (Chapter 5), and his political theory (Chapter 6).

CHAPTER FOUR

On Religion

What Schleiermacher has to say about the phenomenon of religion has been controversial since he published *On Religion: Speeches to Its Cultured Despisers* in 1799. From the theological side he has been criticized for veering too close to pantheism, and for analyzing religion as a universal feature of human nature rather than as a response to (supernatural) revelation. I do not think either criticism is quite fair, but these are topics for Chapter 5. In this chapter I want to look at Schleiermacher's role as a theorist of religion. That role has been important for the academic disciplines that go under the names of religious studies, the history of religions, and comparative religions in the English-speaking world.

Here Schleiermacher's reputation has often faired badly. I think Schleiermacher has a robust theory of religion that has been almost entirely misinterpreted. My goal in this chapter is to give an accurate account of Schleiermacher's theory. I will describe the standard reading of Schleiermacher on religion and why it has become dominant. I will say why I think this account is inaccurate. I will try to give a better account of Schleiermacher on religion. I will end with some thoughts on Schleiermacher's importance for contemporary theory in religious studies.

The Standard Reading

Schleiermacher has been caught in the crossfire of a dispute about proper method in the academic study of religion. The debate is about whether or not religion can and should be explained scientifically. Those who say it can are referred to as "reductionists" by those who disagree with them. Those who say it cannot are labeled, in turn, "theologians." Both are used as terms of abuse in this context. Reductionism in this context refers to a misapplication of scientific method where it does not belong. In the philosophy of science to reduce is to subsume an explanatory theory or set of theories under a more comprehensive theory. But, it is claimed, religion is not a phenomenon like the phenomena studied by the hard sciences. It is not like the motion of objects or the evolution of species, it is sui generis, literally, in a class by itself. One can try to interpret religious phenomena, the way one interprets art and literature, but one cannot explain it. So to "reduce" religious phenomena under theories that come from economics or psychology or sociology or biology is to misplace religion and therefore to rule out a proper account of it from the outset. Religion may be affected by any of these factors (psychological or economic, for example), but it *is* none of them.[1]

"Theologians" are accused of not pursuing academic work at all, no matter how erudite. They do not, it is claimed, play by the normal academic rules of citing publicly available evidence to support their claims. Instead they appeal to something mysterious or ineffable. "Reductionists" claim that religion is in whole or in part a set of human behaviors and beliefs. It therefore ought to be amenable to explanation by the tools developed to explain human behavior. This trajectory of the study of religion has its roots in the Enlightenment's attempt to find a naturalistic explanation for religion.[2] From this perspective, scholars who try to avoid naturalistic explanations of religion in favor of "interpreting" or "understanding" religious phenomena have abdicated their academic responsibilities. Rather than accounting for religious behavior they are in covert ways engaging in apologetics, protecting religion and promoting a certain (usually liberal Protestant) religious worldview.

Schleiermacher is frequently accused by the nontheological side of this debate as being the progenitor of the bad study of religion that is theological and designed to protect and promote rather than explain religion. Wayne Proudfoot argues that "Schleiermacher's conception of religion . . . was intended as a response to Kant's critiques."[3] Russell McCutcheon, for example, writes that Schleiermacher makes religion "a non-quantifiable individual experience, a deep feeling, or an immediate consciousness."[4] This is a protective move to make religion internal and ineffable, not accessible to scientific methods of explanation. Walter Capps, in a textbook widely used in introductory religious studies courses, argues that Schleiermacher defines religion as a kind of feeling or quality, "something akin to a deep sensitivity. Feeling connotes a manner of inwardness, an interior self-consciousness, an awareness of the kind we speak of when we say that something 'moves' us deeply."[5] Eric Sharpe, in another influential history of the discipline, writes that Schleiermacher contributed "a feeling for the irrational in religion."[6] In a discussion of Rudolf Otto, Sharpe writes,

> Another term used by Otto to describe "the faculty, of whatever sort it may be, of genuinely cognizing and recognizing the holy in its appearances" is "divination"—normally used in the more specific sense of receiving communications from the supernatural world. This Otto specifically describes as a "theological discovery," and refers back to the classical Christian doctrine of the witness of the Holy Spirit, . . . the theology of Schleiermacher, and the doctrine of Ahnung as found in J. F. Fries.[7]

One can trace a kind of genealogy in religious studies of this interpretation of Schleiermacher from McCutcheon (2001), Capps (1995), and Sharpe (1975) to Mircea Eliade's *The Sacred and the Profane* (1957), in which Eliade takes as his starting point the work of Rudolf Otto's *The Idea of the Holy* (German 1917). It is in this book that Otto makes the famous statement, "whoever knows no such moments in his experience is requested to read no further."[8] This claim, which implies that religion is not essentially a publicly accessible phenomenon but is rather a private experience with which one can empathize or not according to one's own religious experiences, is a claim against which the nontheological ("reductionist") wing of the study of religions rally. It is taken to embody everything that is wrong with the academic study of religion.[9] Thus Schleiermacher is taken as a symbol of the type of theory of religion associated with Otto and Eliade, and as the originator of the type.[10]

The theorists of religion listed above do not actually expend much energy reading and expositing Schleiermacher himself. I do not fault them for that, since there has to be a division of labor in the academy. When English-speaking theorists of religion want to know something about Schleiermacher they have most often turned to two books, each in its own way excellent and important, by scholars who have done their homework. These books are *The Nature of Doctrine* by the theologian George Lindbeck,[11] and *Religious Experience* by the philosopher of religion Wayne Proudfoot.[12] While each of these books has much to recommend it, they both present a fairly old-fashioned and inaccurate picture of Schleiermacher. This picture is the result in part of Schleiermacher's reception history, in part of the texts readily accessible in the 1980s.

Lindbeck identifies Schleiermacher as the source of what he calls the "experiential-expressivist" theory of doctrine. This theory "interprets [religious] doctrines as noninformative and nondiscursive symbols of inner feelings, attitudes, or existential orientations."[13] Other experiential-expressivists include Otto, Eliade, Paul Tillich, and Bernard Lonergan. Despite differences among these thinkers, according to Lindbeck they all

> locate ultimately significant contact with whatever is finally important to religion in the prereflective experiential depths of the self and regard the public or outer features of religion as expressive and evocative objectifications (i.e., nondiscursive symbols) of internal experience.[14]

The term here with which we will need to concern ourselves below is "prereflective." One of Lindbeck's concerns is with the possibility of ecumenical dialogue, and he notes as an advantage of the experiential-expressivist theory that it opens the possibility that the specific doctrines of different religions may not be making incompatible truth claims. A Buddhist and a Christian "might have basically the same faith, although expressed very differently."[15] But for that to be true requires that a person's inner experience, or at least a person's inner religious experience, be basically free from external cultural or historical influences. This experience would be expressed in language, but if people from different languages and cultures have basically the same experience, it could not be shaped by language or culture. And Lindbeck holds that to be impossible.[16] Lindbeck endorses what he calls a "cultural-linguistic" theory of religion and doctrine, in which one's experiences, including one's religious experiences, are shaped and made possible by one's language and culture. One of the strengths of Lindbeck's book is the strong anthropological and theological case he makes for this cultural-linguistic view. I agree with him that it is a better account of the relationship of experience to religious statements than the experiential-expressivist theory. As I will try to show below, so does Schleiermacher.[17]

Wayne Proudfoot's *Religious Experience* is a theoretically astute classic in the study of religious experience. It raises serious questions about a strand in religious studies that attempts to ground religions on preconceptual, unmediated experience. In addition to Otto and Eliade, Proudfoot puts William James in this orientation of thought. But Proudfoot's analysis of this tradition of thinking about religious experience is based on a reading of Schleiermacher that I think can no longer be sustained. Proudfoot's claims are similar to Lindbeck's and can be summarized as follows. For Schleiermacher:

1. religious consciousness is independent of concepts and beliefs;
2. the moment of religious consciousness can be described as a sense of the infinite or consciousness of absolute dependence (the first phrase is from Schleiermacher's *Speeches*, the second from his *Christian Faith*);
3. religious language is best understood not as propositional assertions but as spontaneous expressions of this basic moment of religious consciousness.[18]

Proudfoot is more concerned with the tradition of religious studies in the United States than Lindbeck, whose primary concern is ecumenical dialogue. But Proudfoot largely agrees with Lindbeck's interpretation of Schleiermacher when he writes that "[o]ur knowledge of our own affective states enables us to understand the linguistic expressions of the emotions of others."[19] And Schleiermacher makes this move, Proudfoot argues, to protect religion from Kantian critique. "Schleiermacher's conception of religion was inspired by the pietistic tradition in which he was nurtured, and it was intended as a response to Kant's critiques."[20] In more recent writings Proudfoot has revised his assessment of Schleiermacher somewhat.[21]

The Sources of this Reading

This way of interpreting Schleiermacher has a long and venerable tradition. Andrew Dole traces the claim that Schleiermacher makes religion into something subjective and private to Hegel:

> In *Faith and Knowledge* Hegel characterized Schleiermacher's religion as "subjective" in the sense that it ideally forms a multitude of separate communities that not only allow each other to hold divergent views of the nature of the Absolute but even tolerate an internal diversity of such views.[22]

Hegel contrasts this view with his own, in which the Absolute is accessible to reason (which Schleiermacher, as we saw in Chapter 2, denies), and is therefore "objective."

The claim that, for Schleiermacher, the appropriate method for studying this subjective phenomenon is not scientific and explanatory but humanistic and interpretive dates back to Wilhelm Dilthey's (1833–1911) appropriation of Schleiermacher for his own methodological work. Dilthey made a basic division between natural sciences and the humanities (*Geisteswissenschaften*, literally "sciences of the spirit"), and held that each had a method appropriate to it. Dilthey argued that, "we explain nature, but we understand mental life." This distinction in method is based on the fact that, for Dilthey, in the natural sciences "facts . . . enter consciousness from without" while in the humanities "facts . . . enter consciousness in an originary way from within." The method of understanding products of the human spirit is fundamentally hermeneutic, and Dilthey points to Schleiermacher's lectures on Hermeneutics as "the origin of a general discipline and methodology of interpretation," "an essential part of the foundation of the *Geisteswissenschaften*."[23]

Dilthey's theorizing of the different methods of the sciences and the humanities has been influential on the way universities set up their departmental structures and curricula (most universities have separate divisions for arts and for sciences, with corresponding undergraduate degrees of BA and BS). Eliade, who was perhaps the most influential historian of religions of the second half of the twentieth century, clearly leans on this distinction when he argues that religion, as sui generis, cannot be explained using the methods of other sciences.

But I think it is a mistake to accept Hegel's characterization of Schleiermacher. We will see below the ways in which religion is very public, for Schleiermacher. As for the proper method of studying religion, I think it is a mistake to conflate Schleiermacher and Dilthey. Returning to Schleiermacher's architectonic of knowledge on page 34 of Chapter 2, we see that Schleiermacher does make a basic division in the sciences between physics, the sciences of nature, and ethics, the sciences of reason. But nature and reason are never divorced for Schleiermacher; they are always implicated in each other. And so it is appropriate that while Schleiermacher distinguishes two methods of study, speculative and empirical, he does not associate the speculative with ethics and the empirical with physics exclusively. The study of ethics and physics each has a speculative and an empirical part. Religion, as one of the individual/symbolizing activities of ethics (see Figure 2.2), will appropriately be studied both speculatively and empirically. As we saw in our chapter on Hermeneutics, the effort to understand the speech acts of others has a grammatical and a technical part. Even the technical part, concerning speech acts as a product of human personality, is based on (empirical) comparisons of what we know about the speaker with what we know about ourselves and other humans we have interpreted. In Schleiermacher's self-understanding, religion is a particular part of the process of ethics along with other phenomena, including economics, physics, sociability, and so on, and the study of religion makes use of the same set of methods as the study of other activities and phenomena.

An important factor in the standard reading of Schleiermacher is the texts themselves. Important texts are much more readily and reliably available in German since the critical edition (*Kritische Gesamtausgabe*) began appearing in the 1980s.[24] Furthermore,

Schleiermacher's language in the *Speeches*, written for poets and artists while in the throes of the Romantic movement, can be described in places as flowery, and can lend itself to misinterpretation. Given the influence of Dilthey and Eliade, and the state of the texts, the dominance of the standard reading of Schleiermacher is not surprising.

A Better Reading

If we read Schleiermacher, not through the eyes of concerns in religious studies surrounding Eliade and his defenders and detractors,[25] but through the eyes of the issues confronting Schleiermacher's own generation,[26] a different picture emerges. I will set out this picture in two steps. Most discussions of Schleiermacher have focused on the second Speech and Schleiermacher's claim that the essence of religion is an intuition of the infinite. First, I want to describe what I think Schleiermacher is doing in that speech. Second, one of the perennial charges against Schleiermacher is that religion, for him, is individual and internal. But a full account of Schleiermacher on religion has to take account of his discussions of the communal and institutional aspects of religion, found in the fourth Speech among other places.

In the second Speech Schleiermacher calls the essence of religion "intuition and feeling," and he writes that where there is religion there is "an astonishing intuition of the infinite."[27] What does he mean by this? Schleiermacher writes, in the famous "nuptial embrace" passage:

> It is as fleeting and transparent as the first scent with which the dew gently caresses the waking flowers, as modest and delicate as a maiden's kiss, as holy and fruitful as a nuptial embrace; indeed, not *like* these, but *is itself* all of these. A manifestation, an event develops quickly and magically into an image of the universe. Even as the beloved and ever-sought-for form fashions itself, my soul flees toward it; I embrace it, not as a shadow, but as the holy essence itself. I lie on the bosom of the infinite world.[28]

It certainly seems as though he is guilty of exactly what some have charged him with: trying to do an end-run around Kantian criticism and piercing the Kantian veil to get to the (divine) thing-in-itself.

Before proceeding any further we need to get clear on what Schleiermacher himself thinks he means when he uses the terms "intuition," "feeling," and "infinite."

In Chapter 2, I pointed out that Kant's definition of "intuition" ("*Anschauung*") does not correspond to how the English term is used colloquially. Kant writes, "An intuition is a representation of the sort which would depend immediately on the presence of an object."[29] When Schleiermacher uses the same word he is often read as making a non-Kantian leap into the divine (this is what Lindbeck's and Proudfoot's language of "prereflective," "preconceptual," and "unmediated" is intended to convey). In other words, Schleiermacher is read as arguing that before we apply concepts we already have some direct experience that gives us insight into the divine. For Kant this is clearly impossible, since experience itself is constituted by the application of concepts.

But Schleiermacher signals quite explicitly that he is using the term "intuition" in the Kantian sense. Schleiermacher writes that intuition "is and always remains something individual, set apart, the immediate perception, nothing more."[30] Intuition is the product of action on us by something outside us.[31] When we touch something we feel pressure and weight on our fingertips. Schleiermacher writes, "[W]hat you thus intuit and perceive is not the nature of things, but their action upon you. What you know or believe about the nature of things lies far beyond the realm of intuition." He calls "knowledge" or "belief" about "the nature of things" not religion but "empty mythology."[32] Schleiermacher does not think that, by intuiting something, we pierce the Kantian veil and have direct contact with a thing-in-itself.

The paragraph quoted above reads in whole:

> I entreat you to become familiar with this concept: intuition of the universe. It is the hinge of my whole speech; it is the highest and most universal formula of religion on the basis of which you should be able to find every place in religion, from which you may determine its essence and its limits. All intuition proceeds from an influence of the intuited on the one who intuits, from an original and independent action of the former, which is then

grasped, apprehended, and conceived by the latter according to one's own nature.[33]

One can understand intuition, for Schleiermacher, as the objective side of experience (the action on us of something outside us). "Feeling" he defines not primarily as emotion but as the subjective side of experience.

> [E]very intuition is, by its very nature, connected with a feeling. Your senses mediate the connection between the object and yourselves; the same influence of the object, which reveals its existence to you, must stimulate them in various ways and produce a change in your inner consciousness.[34]

An object comes into contact with us, and this has effects on us. The first is intuition, the second feeling. They are two sides of the same coin of experience.[35]

One of Schleiermacher's central concerns in the *Speeches* is to distinguish religion from other kinds of human activity. This is important theoretically, as we will see below, and theologically, as we will see in the next chapter. "Religion's essence is neither thinking nor acting, but intuition and feeling."[36] In other words, religion is not primarily a matter of philosophy or speculation about the nature of the universe, nor is it primarily a matter of moral behavior. Note that both these activities are just that: relatively active. The essence of religion is more passive. It is the effect of the universe on us. Thinking and doing are accompanied by religion in the person who has cultivated this feeling, which Schleiermacher sometimes calls piety. But as a matter of conceptual analysis we can distinguish these three human faculties.

Having claimed that Schleiermacher ought to be read as very Kantian in his use of "intuition," I do want to point out one significant difference between Schleiermacher and Kant. For both, experience is constituted by external stimulation but also by the shape given to appearances by the concepts of our understanding. As we saw in Chapter 2, for Kant there are forms of intuition and pure concepts of the understanding that are universal across humans. But for Schleiermacher concepts are always linguistic. So we will not all intuit and experience in the same way because we do not all speak the same language. This is important for two reasons. First, though in the second Speech Schleiermacher does account for the essence of religion in individual terms (he is talking about the way each of us intuits), it would not be accurate to say that this intuition is completely internal and private. Our experience is shaped by our concepts, which are given to us by our language group. I take this to be what Schleiermacher is referring to when he writes that intuition is apprehended "according to one's own nature" in his "hinge of my whole speech" passage quoted above. And this, second, is very important for Schleiermacher when he accounts for the diversity of religions in the world. It will not be the case, *pace* Lindbeck, that we have the same experience but express it differently. Our experience cannot be preconceptual because it cannot be prelinguistic.

Schleiermacher even argues that one can have religion without God.[37] The shape of one's intuitions will vary from person to person. He writes that, "belief in God depends on the direction of the imagination (*Fantasie*)."[38] In religion as in all else we do not experience directly, we experience *as*.

Religion is public then because it is expressed in a shared "language" of speech and movement. The speech and movement of a community into which one is born, and the history of experiences of the community into which one is born, in turn shapes the religious intuitions and very personality possible for a given individual. On this reading Schleiermacher stands much closer to Lindbeck's cultural-linguistic model than he does to the experiential-expressivist model. We can share in the religious experiences of others, not because our experiences are the same, but because translation, while never perfect, is possible.

Here we need to say a little more about how Schleiermacher uses "intuition." On the one hand, every experience is an intuition, and in every intuition one senses (though one may not pay attention to this) the infinite. On the other hand, there are certain intuitions that are so powerful that they form the basis that gives shape and order to other intuitions. It is these intuitions that Schleiermacher holds give rise to religions.

These basic intuitions will be shaped by culture and language. For example, depending on one's worldview, one might perceive the universe as a system, or as a set of apparently contradictory elements, or as chaotic.³⁹ Schleiermacher ranks these intuitions from higher to lower. The first will eventually be articulated in religious language as monotheism, the second as polytheism.

Some people, called by Schleiermacher virtuosi, have and are aware of these basic intuitions of the infinite. These people are few and far between. Most of us are given or "catch" basic, organizing intuitions from the religious communities in which we are raised. A religious community is a community precisely because of the shared language and way of life that gives it a common spirit. They shape us the way our people (*Volk*) shapes us. Schleiermacher writes in the *Dialectic*:

> Each people [*Volk*] insofar as it is one through language, constitution, way of life, etc., is a true reality of the living power, and the individuals of the people are individual appearances of it, and the essence of the character of the people appears completely in all individuals in an entire period.⁴⁰

People tend to flock to virtuosi. They are charismatic by virtue of their profound intuition. Most people are in a sense parasitic on the intuitions of others.⁴¹

If intuition is not an uncanny leap into the divine abyss but the action on us of something external to us, and feeling is not emotion but the subjective side of intuition, what does it mean to intuit the infinite? Infinite could mean "indefinite," as in a series that never ends. Alternatively it could mean "beyond the finite," as in something (supernatural) of a wholly different order than the natural world. In that case a sense of the infinite would be very close to what Otto means when he writes of the *myterium tremendum*, the awful sense of something supernatural.

I believe Schleiermacher uses "infinite" in neither of those two senses. He writes, "[e]verything finite exists only through the determination of its limits, which must, as it were, 'be cut out of' the infinite."⁴² By "infinite" he means something like the totality of everything that is. Each finite thing that makes up a part of this totality is not independent of the totality. Each finite thing is what it is because it is not any other finite thing. It is affected by, even effected by, every other finite thing in the totality, more or less, depending on how closely or distantly it is related to every other thing.[43]

> See how repulsion and attraction determine everything and are uninterruptedly active everywhere, how all diversity and all opposition are only apparent and relative, and all individuality is merely an empty name. See how all likeness strives to conceal itself and to divide into a thousand diverse forms, and how nowhere do you find something simple, but everything is ornately connected and intertwined.[44]

To have a sense of the infinite in the finite is to experience not just an object's effect on us but the place that object holds in the totality that is our universe. We typically do not pay any attention to this aspect of our experiences, but it is there in principle in every experience. And, Schleiermacher will argue, we can cultivate our ability to pay heed to these connections.

This is why science, far from being a threat to religion, something from which religion requires the protection of the internal and ineffable, is for Schleiermacher a great aid to religion. Science shows us the law-like connection between things, and so makes our experience of the infinite even richer and profounder.

> Certainly a greater yield is vouchsafed to us who have been permitted by a richer age to penetrate deeper into nature's interior. Its chemical powers, the eternal laws according to which bodies themselves are formed and destroyed, these are the phenomena in which we intuit the universe most clearly and in a most holy manner.[45]

On the standard reading of Schleiermacher, he makes religion a matter of feeling rather than knowing or doing in order to shield religion from the Kantian critique that none of our experience is direct, it is all shaped by our minds, and to shield religion from being studied or "reduced" using the methods appropriate to the natural sciences. But on a fresh reading we see that Schleiermacher thinks religion helped, not hurt, by science. And Schleiermacher agrees with Kant that we cannot intuit the thing-in-itself, we do not get a preconceptual experience of the divine. In this sense

Schleiermacher is not a mystic. Schleiermacher's "nuptial embrace" is not a flight from Kantianism but a poetic description of everyday epistemology.

But one could say that Schleiermacher does give us a "something more" in intuition than Kant does. Neither gives us access to the thing-in-itself, but for Kant our experience is an experience of an appearance. For Schleiermacher this appearance is related to every other possible appearance that constitutes our world. When we intuit the infinite we experience something outside of ourselves affecting us, and also a sense that this something is connected causally to everything else. We get a sense of the whole.

So much for the standard misreading of the second Speech. Equally important is the fact that many interpreters have taken that Speech to constitute Schleiermacher's entire theory of religion. But Schleiermacher is adamant that religion is necessarily social, and so to complete his theory of religion we must turn to the fourth Speech, among other materials.

Schleiermacher writes,

> When an individual has produced and formulated something in him or herself, it is pathological and most unnatural to wish to close it up inside him or herself. He or she should express and communicate all that is in him or herself in the indispensible community and mutual dependence of action.[46]

Such expression is a fundamental part of what it is to be human for Schleiermacher, as we saw at the end of Chapter 2. While humans share universal reason, "still higher" for Schleiermacher is "the unique nature which freedom chooses for herself in each individual."[47] This is the expressivist self.

Expressing deeply felt religious affections accomplishes at least two things. First, memory requires that such arousal be expressed in word or deed.[48] "[A]fter every flight of their spirit to the infinite they must set down in pictures or words the impressions it made on them as an object so as to enjoy it themselves afresh."[49]

Second, if religion is essentially a sense or taste of the infinite, one can by definition grasp only a small part of it, intuit it only from a limited perspective. Those who have had intense experiences of the infinite have a desire, not only to express these experiences, but to share in the expressions of others' experiences.

> They are conscious of encompassing only a small part of it, and that which they cannot reach directly they will, at least so far as they are able, take in and enjoy through the representations of others who have appropriated it. Therefore they urge themselves to every expression of the same, and seeking their completion listen for every sound they recognize as religious.[50]

So while it is the case for Schleiermacher that the essence is an intuition and feeling of the infinite, it is also the case that a complete account of Schleiermacher on religion requires an analysis of the social nature of religion.

Andrew Dole proposes a helpful way of organizing the various kinds of statements Schleiermacher makes about religion into three categories.[51] Dole argues that by "religion" Schleiermacher sometimes refers, first, to "interior ideal religion," the essence of religion that is the intuition of the infinite in the finite. Second, Schleiermacher sometimes refers to "external ideal religion," the religion of "activities, artifacts, or states of affairs."[52] These activities have mostly to do with communication. One naturally expresses important experiences, and one naturally wants to share these expressions with others, and share in theirs. These are the kinds of things we have been considering here in our discussion of the fourth Speech. Third, Schleiermacher sometimes refers to "actual religion," the religion that we find in history embodied in institutions.

It is important to be as clear as possible on the way Schleiermacher uses the concept of essence. Dole argues that essences traditionally served both an explanatory role (they make something what it is) and a classificatory role (they are the *sine qua non* that allows us to classify things).[53] But Dole claims that Schleiermacher does not use essence in exactly this way. By essence Schleiermacher means not something explanatory and classificatory, but something closer to Ernst Troeltsch's (1865–1923) use of the concept. Troeltsch writes,

> With respect to all of these the conception of the essence is at the same time a criticism. It is not merely an abstraction from

the manifestations, but at the same time a criticism of the manifestations, and this criticism is not merely an evaluation of that which is not yet complete in terms of the driving ideal, but a discrimination between that which corresponds to the essence and that which is contrary to it.[54]

The essence provides criteria by which to judge the historical development of traditions and to determine the extent to which these developments are in accord with the internal ideal. To the extent they are in accord these developments will be externally ideal. But Schleiermacher is very aware that religions, in their historical development, often diverge or fall short of this ideal. Thus the essence of religion does not constitute the whole of religion, rather it provides a criterion by which actual religion can be analyzed and criticized.

This does seem to be pretty close to what Schleiermacher is up to in the *Speeches*. Schleiermacher writes that where there is religion there is "an astonishing intuition of the infinite." This is the essence, or internal ideal, of religion. These intuitions naturally give rise to expressions in word and gesture. Communities form around these expressions for the purpose of sharing and strengthening these experiences. Such communities are necessary for the preservation and cultivation of religious experiences. This is the external ideal of religion. This external ideal provides Schleiermacher with criteria by which to judge the quality of religious communities. Recall Schleiermacher's expressivist commitment:

> [E]ach should grant to the other freedom to go where the spirit drives him or her, and be helpful only where the other feels a lack, not attributing to the other his or her own thoughts. In this way each would find in the other life and nourishment, and that which each could become, he or she would become fully.[55]

One's piety, while internal, can only develop in relationship with others.[56] Communities that facilitate this free exchange of expression approach the external ideal. Communities that do not facilitate this free exchange of expression fall short. The external ideal of a religious community, then, will be free from external interference, will be radically egalitarian, and will be focused on communication. As Dole writes,

> An ideal religious community will be one characterized by patterns of social interaction that represent optimal collective activity in relation to the sort of thing an essence of religion is. Schleiermacher's conception of ideal religious community in the Speeches was in fact predicated on the idea that there is one particular social pattern or social form that most adequately corresponds to religion's essence. We can understand this social form as religiously inflected free sociability.[57]

Free sociability is a social form of the mutual exchange of thought and expression, perhaps best exemplified in the Berlin salons. Religiously inflected free sociability occurs when the content of such exchanges is restricted to religious topics. This is the form religious communities take when they develop in accordance with their internal ideal.

Schleiermacher is well aware that existing religious communities, actual religion, are a mixed bag. They have elements of ideal internal and external religion, but also fall short of ideal religion. And he has an account (an explanation!) of the factors that can lead a religious tradition away from the ideal.

Religions can degenerate if what were originally expressions of powerful intuitions begin to be mindlessly repeated, either in verbal formulas or in ritual. If this happens the religion can ossify, the external expressions no longer communicate something lively. Without external expressions the internal intuitions themselves begin to weaken. In Schleiermacher's opinion this is what has happened to the Orthodox Judaism of his day. In language that can only make us cringe today, Schleiermacher writes, "Judaism is long since a dead religion, and those who at present still bear its colors are actually sitting and mourning beside the undecaying mummy and weeping over its demise and its sad legacy."[58]

Religions can also be contaminated by nonreligious elements. This can happen internally. Since religion and philosophy, according to Schleiermacher, both are related to the same object (the whole), it is easy for people to get sidetracked from the experience of the infinite onto useless speculation about the infinite. Contamination can also occur from the outside, when the state tries to harness religion to achieve its own ends. In Prussia ministers were civil servants, employed by the state. It was natural for the state to try to use churches to inculcate the moral values useful to it. But Schleiermacher has carefully distinguished morals from religion. Too much state interference will inhibit the free exchange of pious feelings.

To be sure, Schleiermacher sometimes talks as though what I have called here "actual religion" is not really religion. In the first Speech in particular, when he is trying to convince the cultured despisers that what they commonly think of as religion (mindlessly repeated formulas, tyrannical priests) is not what religion is, he sometimes writes that what I am here calling actual religion is not religion at all. But, as Dole points out, it is disingenuous of later scholars to adopt Schleiermacher's definition of religion's essence (intuition of the infinite), and then judge what Schleiermacher has to say about religion using their own definition of religion as public and historical, as if Schleiermacher has nothing to say about the public, social aspects of religion. Schleiermacher gives a robust account of these aspects of what most of us call religion, and provides theories on how religion in this sense develops. An assessment of his theory of religion, then, should not overlook that account.

Two things remain in this account of Schleiermacher on religion. First, it is typical in discussing this topic to address the Introduction to his *Christian Faith* in relationship to the *Speeches*. I am going to postpone this discussion to the next chapter, "Mediating Theology," where the *Christian Faith* will be the central text. Here I will simply note that I think he gives largely the same account in both places, but his language has shifted some over the years, and he is writing very intentionally to a very different audience.

Second, I owe some assessment of whether or not this is a good theory of religion. Here my reflections will not be tied as closely to the reading of specific texts as they otherwise are in this book, and will be more wide-ranging and personal. Schleiermacher's theory is surely a better one than he has been given credit for. I think it is important to pay attention to the insights Schleiermacher offers into the dynamics of historical traditions. If Isaiah Berlin is correct that the expressivist self has become the modern anthropology, then Schleiermacher's account of the linguistic nature of humans, and his account of how communities form, shape, and are shaped by individuals is an astute analysis. Following from that, I think he has usefully identified some of the dynamics in the growth, healthy or not, of religious communities.

Schleiermacher's account of religion, as originating in a natural feature of regular human cognition, is in line with one of the growth industries in religious studies today, the cognitive science of religion. This field argues that religion develops out of natural cognitive processes that have developed over human history. Schleiermacher's specific account of the cognitive processes, of course, is a very nineteenth-century one, and different from the kinds of processes studied by cognitive sciences today. But both are attempts to make possible naturalistic explanations of religious thought and behavior.

If Schleiermacher as theorist of religion scores better than expected, there are still reasons to be restrained in praising his contributions. He is a very far-sighted nineteenth-century figure, but a nineteenth-century figure nonetheless. Dole has contributed to a sophisticated assessment of Schleiermacher on the essence of religion. Certainly I hope to have shown that what Schleiermacher means by essence is not a defensive, anticritical or antiscientific move. But any discussion of religion's essence will sound, to many contemporary students of religion, old-fashioned.

One way to sort out the issues here is to turn to a famous declaration by one of the most prominent recent theorists of religion, Jonathan Z. Smith, who has written that "religion is solely the creation of the scholar's study."[59] If, by this, Smith means that religion did not exist until the academic project of trying to explain it developed during the Enlightenment, then this is clearly a silly position. "Religion," while not a universal category, is an emic category in many cultures, one with a long history. But Smith's point is that, in defining "religion," a scholar's task is not to take "religion" as given and attempt to get the best fix possible on what religion is. For Smith, religion is a constructed, not natural, category. Schleiermacher is a "realist" about the category religion. For him religion exists in the world independent of scholars of religion. Thus he distinguishes religion from metaphysics and morals. For Smith, in contrast, the scholar defines religion, and takes ownership of that definition, because it is up to the scholar to decide what is useful and illuminating to compare. Thus Smith can avoid endless debates about the accuracy or correctness of different attempts to define religion, attempts to match our definition with what exists in the world independently of the definition. Is Theravada Buddhism a religion? Is communism? Is vegetarianism? To use essences is to expect a yes or no (or, in the most sophisticated cases, a graded) answer. And this answer will be right or wrong. Smith's point is that, if a useful comparison can be made between Levitical food laws and contemporary eating practices, then define "religion" in such a way that these can be brought under the same category. But the scholar's next project (cult of the saints and cult of the great leader, for example) may have different comparative contours, and so the definition will shift. It is in this sense that the scholar self-consciously creates "religion" each time he or she makes a comparison.

The issues here are complex, but Smith's strategy seems to me to be a more fruitful way to approach the disciplinary task of defining religion than endless debates about the merits of certain attempts at definition. Schleiermacher, like the rest of his century, like many undergraduates, and like some of the less sophisticated cognitive scientists of religion, would be puzzled by Smith's approach.

One of the most pressing recent tasks in religious studies has been the turn to genealogy. If it is not the case that religion naturally is something, yet it is also the case that religion is an emic term in Europe and the United States, such that if you ask most people on the street what they think religion is they will have no trouble giving you an answer (unless they have had a course in religious studies), what is the history of this term? What category does it circumscribe, and how has that category shifted over time?

"Religion" does have a history, and here I think Schleiermacher's theoretical contributions to the study of religion cannot be overestimated. Schleiermacher is one of the earliest theorists to historicize religion, to argue that it is not a generic category but an abstraction from historical (what he calls "positive religion") traditions. And he can account for typical ways in which these traditions develop.

There is a second sense in which Schleiermacher's influence in the history of the category of religion cannot be overestimated. I think he had a profound influence on what most people in liberal nations take religion to be (I use "liberal" here not in contrast to "conservative" but in the sense in which all Western nations are constitutional republics, that is, politically liberal). Religion is typically taken to be a matter of conscience, something that ought not in principle to be coerced. This is why, in the United States, one can give religious reasons to be classified as a "conscientious objector" and be freed from having to register for the military draft. Freedom of religion is protected as the first right in the Bill of Rights of the US constitution. But to point this out is to point out that, in a sense, Schleiermacher has won the argument of the *Speeches*. Religion is not external authority and priests and rituals (Speech One). Religion is a matter of personal insight or feeling (Speech Two) shared in and organized by community (Speech Four).[60] In other words, to the extent that people take a realist stance toward religion, to the extent that they assume that religion is a real thing in the world independent of scholarly definitions, I think they mean something by the word religion largely in line with what Schleiermacher means by it. But this is not exactly the same category as denoted by the word religion and its cognates in the West up through the Enlightenment.

Schleiermacher did not accomplish this shift in essential definition of religion single-handedly, of course, but he was one of the most prominent and articulate advocates for this shift. His way of creating categories of human activities in the *Philosophical Ethics*[61] is a kind of blueprint for distinguishing modern religion from politics and economics, from science and education, and for thinking about how religious activities ought properly to relate to activities in these other categories.[62] One effect of his careful distinction of religious activity from political and economic activity is that, in the wake of Schleiermacher, it becomes possible to conceive of religious identity apart from ethnic or cultural identity. Schleiermacher, for example, was one of the foremost advocates for full citizenship of Jews in Prussia without linking citizenship to religious conversion.[63]

Here an examination of Schleiermacher on religion is extremely important for scholars of religion. There is much that is appealing in Schleiermacher's theories: it makes religion dovetail nicely with the anthropology of expressivism that we have discussed; it is an appealing account of the personal and communal aspects of religion; it is an appealing account of religion's relationship to other spheres of human activity. But there is an unavoidable valuation of religions that is entailed by Schleiermacher's theories.[64] Dole is right that ideal external religion, the proper development of religion in accord with its internal essence, is for Schleiermacher an ideal linked to free sociability. Religions that promote free expression and discourage external interference, minimize rote repetition, and see themselves as cultivating personal insight, will be intrinsically *better* religions. They will resemble the middle-class salons of turn of the (nineteenth-) century Berlin. If Schleiermacher is an important figure in the construction of modern religion, as I have argued, then scholars of religion will have to be conscious of the imbedded normative judgments that are entailed by our modern category, as we do our comparative work of religions from different historical eras and different cultures and languages. I do not advocate getting rid of the category of religion, as some scholars have, nor do I think scholars of religion need to avoid normative judgments. But I think responsible use of the category requires that we make very explicit the historical link of our category to a certain moment middle-class European development.[65]

In discussing Schleiermacher as a theorist of religion I have leaned heavily on previous chapters to show that, far from trying to protect religion from Enlightenment critiques, Schleiermacher embraces those critiques to give an account of religion that is natural, social, and historical. In the next chapter I turn to Schleiermacher, not as theorist of religion, but as someone training intellectual leaders of a specific religion. While Schleiermacher is quite careful to distinguish these two tasks, having seen what he has to say about religion will allow us to move quickly to some of his most important theological positions.

CHAPTER FIVE

Mediating Theology

I have been concerned in the preceding chapters (and will be again, in Chapter 6) to show the range of fields in which Schleiermacher made important contributions. This has been a pressing task, since much of the literature available in English about him has focused on his theology. But of course it is as a theologian that he is most famous, and justly so, and so we turn in this chapter to his primary theological commitments, and how they play out in several central Christian doctrines. There are many fine systematic theologies, but Schleiermacher's *The Christian Faith* ranks among Thomas's *Summa Theologiae*, Calvin's *Institutes of the Christian Religion*, and Barth's *Church Dogmatics* in its profundity, comprehensiveness, and epoch-making effect.

It turns out that our time spent outside theology proper has been time well-spent, because a knowledge of ethics, dialectic, hermeneutics, theory of religion, and so on will facilitate an efficient and nuanced understanding of some of the theological moves Schleiermacher makes, moves that sometimes throw his readers into confusion. I will proceed by saying what theology, for Schleiermacher, is; I will give an overview of how he conceptualizes the various theological disciplines; I will take, as an example of an important doctrine (the important doctrine, for Schleiermacher), his Christology; I will discuss the controversial Introduction to *The Christian Faith*; and then I will turn to the doctrines of sin and redemption.

What Is Theology?

Schleiermacher's youth included a painful chapter in which he left the Moravian seminary, and exchanged a series of difficult letters with his father. As we saw in Chapter 1, the issue revolved around certain doctrinal expressions of faith. Though Schleiermacher loved the Moravian community and experienced a conversion there, as a matter of conscience he could not subscribe to the theories of the dual natures of Christ and the vicarious atonement. His father, for whom faith required specific propositional truth assertions (Jesus has two natures; Jesus' death appeased a wrathful God), reacted badly. But later, on a return visit to the Moravians, Schleiermacher records that he has become a Moravian again, "of a higher order." What we see in this story is a firm distinction that Schleiermacher will come to make throughout his life between religion and theology. Religion does not equal correct theology. Religion is not first and foremost a set of propositional assertions about the world. Religion in essence is an experience of the infinite. For Christians, religion is the experience of redemption found in the Christian community. That is the key thing for Schleiermacher. Theology is an attempt to express this experience in as adequate a language as possible. As B. A. Gerrish noted of the youthful Schleiermacher among the Moravians, "what Schleiermacher lost was not his faith in Christ but his first understanding of it."[1] Faith, and the way faith is best expressed, are not the same thing. Theology has many important uses for Schleiermacher but is always secondary to, and not to be confused with, Christian faith.

In *The Christian Faith* Schleiermacher sets out a sophisticated theory of language that adds some nuance to the way I have formulated "theology" above.[2] He distinguishes three kinds of religious speech. The first is poetic. Poetic speech is "based originally on a moment of enthusiasm that has come from within." Its goal is purely representational. It brings out into the world an inner feeling.[3] Poetic speech is the natural form of speech when one is in the grips of an intense experience of the infinite.

The second form of speech described by Schleiermacher is rhetorical. This is the speech of preaching. It is based on "a moment of moved interest whose intensification has come from without." Recall that those who have experienced the infinite are eager to learn of the experience of others. This prompting to tell us about your experience is the intensification from without. The goal of rhetorical speech is "stimulative," that is it tries to bring hearers to the same aroused consciousness as the speaker. Schleiermacher calls both the poetic and rhetorical forms of speech "original."

The third form of speech is descriptively didactic (*darstellend belehrend*). One uses this form of speech when one wishes to make the first two forms of speech as precise and comprehensible to others as possible. This is the language of instruction, not preaching. When one is doing systematic theology, "in which the highest possible degree of definiteness is aimed at,"[4] this is the form of language best suited to specifying doctrine.

It is important to follow the correct order in doing theology in Schleiermacher's idiom. His *The Christian Faith* is written for those who are already members of the Christian community (more specifically he is writing for those who are members of the unified Reformed/Lutheran Prussian Protestant community). He is not trying to prove any propositions about the world; rather he is assuming a common experience. (In today's parlance he is a "nonfoundationalist.") His students are training to become church leaders, and so will be aided by being able to articulate expressions of their belief with as much clarity as possible. And when one puts first-order poetic and rhetorical religious expressions into second-order descriptively didactic language, the inner connection between the doctrines becomes apparent. Order is not imposed on the doctrines, but their natural order is made clear. We can now see why Schleiermacher titles his book *The Christian Faith According to the Principles of the Evangelical Church Presented in Their Connection* (*Zusammenhange*—literally "hanging-together"). We can also see why it was important for Schleiermacher to include on the title page a quote from Anselm (omitted from the title page of the English translation): "I do not seek to understand in order that I may believe, but I believe in order that I may understand. . . . For anyone who has not believed will not experience, and anyone who has not experienced will not understand." We see why the notes in this book very frequently cite creedal statements rather than Scripture—all Christians share Scripture, but Schleiermacher is articulating the experience of faith in a particular Christian community (the evangelical community), who have defined themselves as a particular community in large part through creeds.⁵ And we can see why Schleiermacher refers to his undertaking as "dogmatics," a word as unfashionable in his day as it is in ours. Schleiermacher often refers to his book as the *Glaubenslehre* (as do scholars working with this text), which translates roughly as "doctrine of faith." He sees his project as articulating the faith of the community in scientifically precise language.

To undertake theology as an explication of the faith found in the community is Schleiermacher's fundamental theological move. It is this move, this turn to a "theology of consciousness," and the skill with which he executes it, that earns him the epitaph "father of modern theology." Before going in to more detail, I want simply to point out some of the advantages and ramifications of this move.

Schleiermacher lives in the wake of the Enlightenment. Two of the greatest challenges left by the Enlightenment for Christian theology were the rise of science and the rise of the historical consciousness. Both are rooted in a shifting epistemology and new criteria for legitimate epistemological authority. The scientific view of the world called into question the plausibility of some of the biblical accounts. If Newton's equations accurately describe the motion of all objects in the universe, is there room for divine intervention that disrupts the laws? And should we pursue answers to a question like this by reference to ancient texts, or by reference to the evidence of the world itself? Even more troubling, ultimately, were the questions raised by history. By what right do we treat the Bible as a book different from other ancient books? How do we determine who the human authors of the texts were? Can we assume they are addressing the same concerns that we bring to the text from our different context? And how do we assess the reliability of these human authors as historical witnesses?

By defining religion as a matter of experience (feeling) rather than a matter of knowing, like natural science and philosophy, or morals, and by defining dogmatic theology as a second-order expression of religious experience, Schleiermacher declares some of the most troubling of these questions to be a category mistake. Science and religion have an "eternal covenant," a nonaggression pact, because each uses its own methods to undertake different tasks, tasks that do not overlap. And the historical examination of the biblical texts does not threaten Christian faith. The Bible holds a special place for Schleiermacher because it is the first recorded expression of Christian experience. But it is that experience, the experience of redemption found in the Christian community, that is the source of faith and the bedrock of theology. If it turns out that we know less than we thought we did about certain events or certain authors, that does not call into question that experience of faith found in the community. I do not think that these challenges to theology have changed since Schleiermacher's day, and schools of theology that have found Schleiermacher inadequate ignore these problems at their own peril. Schleiermacher's ability to put theology on a new footing while maintaining continuity with the core Protestant experience and language of "justification by faith" have led B. A. Gerrish and Walter Wyman to label him a "liberal evangelical."[6]

The Field of Theology

Before turning to specific dogmas it will be useful to see the place that dogmatic theology holds in Schleiermacher's architectonic of the overall field of theology. Schleiermacher lectured on "Theological Encyclopedia," a term common in his day for an overview of the structure of a field, from 1805–06 in Halle to 1831–32 in Berlin, a total of 11 times.[7] In 1811 he published the notes for these lectures in an important book titled *Brief Outline of the Study of Theology*.[8] Students in seminary will already be familiar with this book even if they have not heard of it, for many of Schleiermacher's ideas for a seminary curriculum have become institutionalized and seem today to be simple common sense (though the book contains at least one significant surprise I will discuss below). As noted in Chapter 1, Schleiermacher helped create the University of Berlin and was appointed the first dean of the theology faculty, and so had a chance to build that curriculum according to his ideas.

Schleiermacher divides theology into a threefold structure of philosophical, historical, and practical theology. Schleiermacher's dogmatics can appear esoteric (in his university all the theology students would already have studied a fair amount of philosophy, and so Schleiermacher does not shy away from technical language).

So in order to understand his priorities it is crucial to point out that, for him, practical theology is the crown of the theological disciplines. Referring back to Figure 2.1 in Chapter 2, practical theology is a technical science—it is intended to teach people techniques to do something.[9] Theology in general is for the sake of training church leaders, and practical theology gives them the techniques to take what they learn in all theological disciplines and further the ends of the church.

Philosophical theology is in the service of practical theology. It "presents the essence of Christianity, that by which it is a distinctive mode of faith."[10] One must be in a position to say what a religion is, what distinguishes it from other kinds of activities (refer here to Figure 2.2 from Chapter 2, showing the outline of human activities from the Philosophical Ethics). Having said what religion is, one must then be able to articulate what distinguishes Christianity from other religions.

Finally we come to historical theology, which Schleiermacher further subdivides into (1) exegetical theology (the study of primitive Christianity's normative documents), (2) church history, and (3) the church in its contemporary historical moment.[11] It is here, as the contemporary historical moment of the church, that Schleiermacher locates dogmatic theology. This is the surprise I mentioned above. It struck many in Schleiermacher's day, as it does in ours, as an odd way to conceive of dogmatics. Many people assume that theology is a closer relative to philosophy than to history, though perhaps with an adjusted set of presuppositions. Theology sounds like propositional truth claims about the world, and the task of theology can seem, like that of philosophy, to be to assess the warrants and justifications for these truth claims, to defend them, and to argue for their superiority against competing truth claims. But this is precisely what theology need not do, according to Schleiermacher, since (and here he does sound a lot like Lindbeck) theology is undertaken by those who share an experience and language. One can argue with other theologians about whether or not a development is in line with the essence of the community's experience (this is where preparatory work in philosophical theology comes into play), and one can argue about the adequacy of second-order articulations of that experience, but the experience itself is not up for grabs.

Christology

I want now to give an example of a doctrine or dogma as we see it in *The Christian Faith*. Who is Jesus and how does he effect our salvation? What is the work of Christ?[12] (I will have more to say below on what salvation is; here I want to focus on how this salvation is mediated to us through Jesus, according to Schleiermacher.)

Schleiermacher's generation found itself confronted with two ways of approaching answers to these questions. These ways will seem very familiar to contemporary readers. Schleiermacher was satisfied with neither. On the one side Schleiermacher found a group of confessionalists, traditionalists who emphasized correct doctrine, and pietists emphasizing conversion and a personal relationship to God. For these people Jesus effects our salvation supernaturally. Though crucified and resurrected Jesus can still intervene in the causal nexus of our universe to accomplish his goals in a way that is beyond and inexplicable by that causal nexus. Schleiermacher calls such a view "magical." The strength of this view is its connection to the traditional language of Christianity, and its ability to talk about a very real presence of Jesus in our lives. Its weakness is that it seemed to Schleiermacher to call for a sacrifice of the intellect, to ask us to deny all the best fruits of the human intellectual and cultural endeavors that were so exciting and empowering in his day. The traditionalists acknowledged that it may be harder in the modern world, after Newton and the scientific successes of the empirical method, to believe the miraculous accounts of Scripture. But that was too bad for the modern world, not for Scripture. Salvation required precisely believing the unbelievable.

On the other side Schleiermacher found a group of rationalists and deists of various stripes. Jesus was seen by them as a great moral teacher, perhaps the greatest moral teacher, who not only taught turning the other cheek and the Golden Rule and helping the sick and poor and outcast, but followed his own precepts unto death. We can learn from Jesus' teachings, and follow his example, but Jesus is dead, no longer present. Schleiermacher calls this view "empirical." The strength of this view is that it does not require one to choose between scientific and philosophical advances and Jesus. Its weakness is that it is not really a religion. It is a set of moral ideas. There is no ongoing role for or presence of Jesus—he is crucified and gone.

Schleiermacher's way out of this untenable choice is to formulate a third way with the strengths of both and the weaknesses of neither. What is it that Jesus does? Jesus founds a community. Because of the strength and charisma of his personality, people flocked to Jesus. Who is Jesus? The critical aspect of Jesus' personality, according to Schleiermacher, was his perfect God-consciousness, about which I will say more below. All communities, Schleiermacher holds, from families to nations to religions, are founded around the personalities that originally comprised them. We saw how this happened in our discussion in Chapters 2 and 3 of the Dialectic and the Hermeneutics. By sharing our speech and gestures we begin to influence each other and form a group consciousness.

What is distinct in Christianity is not that it formed this way; rather what is distinct is that this is the community that has formed around the personality of this specific individual, Jesus. We saw in Chapter 4 (Theory of Religion) how people, by their social natures, are driven to express their profound religious experiences and how people are driven to listen to and partake in these expressions. We saw in Chapter 3 how language, broadly construed, is the medium of expression, but also how expressions stamped by individual personalities can change the language available to others. And we saw in Chapter 2 that the very concepts, the very mental apparatus that gives to us the active or intellectual part with which we constitute perception and experience, are linguistic concepts.

In other words, as Jesus expresses his experience to others, they begin to adopt his way of speaking and gesturing, his facial expressions. This, too, we see in all communities. One can easily observe how groups of friends begin to adopt some of each other's word choices, mannerisms, and speech patterns. In adopting the speech and mannerisms of Jesus, new conceptual horizons and therefore new possibilities of experience open up for his followers. Jesus used new expressions, and used old ones in new ways. One can think of Christianity as a linguistic revolution.

What was redemptive for the disciples who were face-to-face with Jesus was his personality and the power of his God-consciousness. Gerrish writes, "Schleiermacher thinks that if Christians search their actual experience of the Redeemer, his activity will be seen to resemble the attractive power of a strong personality."[13] The Christian community, formed by Jesus (I choose the word "form" intentionally, trying to recall all the depth and connotations of the German word *Bildung* that we discussed in talking about expressivism and the way people develop into themselves), continues to embody his ways of speaking, gesturing, experiencing. The Christian community carries in it the picture (*Bild*) of Jesus. And so, when latter day people enter into that community they are confronted, in just the way the disciples were, by the redemptive personality of Jesus.

Schleiermacher has found a way to think, in natural terms, about the ongoing presence of Jesus and the redeeming effects of that presence. As Walter Wyman nicely phrases it,

> neither supernaturalism's grace without a mechanism, nor rationalism's religion without the communication of grace, will do. Transforming power is conveyed by the words of the preacher (what could be more classically Protestant than Schleiermacher's emphasis on the Word?) and in the lives of other believers.[14]

The essence of Christianity, for Schleiermacher, is exactly this experience of redemption. It is not a set of intellectual propositions about the world to which one must subscribe. Recall, from our discussion of the *Speeches* in Chapter 4, that religion for Schleiermacher is not thinking or doing, not metaphysics or morality, but feeling. The Christian religion is an experience of redemption linked to the person Jesus. The advantages of this third, "mediating" way are, on the one hand, that it can articulate a very real ongoing presence of Christ. On the other hand, in so doing, it does not require Christians to contradict what they know to be the case about natural systems of causality in other realms of their experience.

Introduction to Christian Faith

I promised, in Chapter 4, a discussion of the Introduction to *The Christian Faith*, and now is the appropriate place to make good on that promise. The Introduction is important for at least three reasons. First, it will give us a better idea of what Schleiermacher means when he talks about "God-consciousness," which, as we saw above, he claims Jesus possessed perfectly. It will round out our discussion of Christology. Second, the Introduction has been the subject of great theological controversy from the time it was first published to the present day. To get an accurate sense of what Schleiermacher thinks he is doing in his *Glaubenslehre*, we will have to address this controversy. Third, the Introduction has also been one of the key texts, along with the *Speeches*, to which theorists of religion have turned when assessing Schleiermacher's account of religion. A discussion of the Introduction will be useful in assessing whether or not they, and I, have been fair to Schleiermacher in considering him as a theorist of religion.

In the Introduction, Schleiermacher offers a description of humans and their relationship to the world that will be familiar to us from the Dialectic and the Ethics. Humans are relatively active, and relatively passive. We act on the world, and the world acts on us.

> Thus in every self-consciousness there are two elements, which we might call respectively a self-caused element (*ein Sichselbstsetzen*) and a non-self-caused element (*ein Sichselbstnichtsogesetzthaben*). . . . Now to these two elements, as they exist together in the temporal self-consciousness, correspond in the subject to its Receptivity and its (spontaneous) Activity.[15]

Schleiermacher thinks this is clear to anyone "capable of a little introspection."

In epistemology, we have an intellectual and an organic side—our experience is the result of our (actively) ordering through concepts (passively) received stimuli. And as subjects we are constantly acting on the world and being acted on by the world. As a result we have a feeling of freedom (when we act) and a feeling of dependence (when we are acted on).

Humans do not, Schleiermacher claims, have a feeling of *absolute* freedom. Even when acting we are aware that we do not create our own existence, but that existence is given to us. We do have a sense of *absolute* dependence:

> [T]he self-consciousness which accompanies all our activity, and therefore, since that is never zero, accompanies our whole existence, and negatives absolute freedom, is itself precisely a

consciousness of absolute dependence; for it is the consciousness that the whole of our spontaneous activity comes from a source outside us.[16]

We have a sense of the givenness of our existence, that we are, as some philosophers have said, "thrown" into existence. I take this to be the same claim, in different language, that Schleiermacher made in the second Speech when he wrote that in every intuition we have also a sense of the infinite in the finite. We experience not just an object but, if we are paying attention, we sense also that the object is part of a whole. We are part of this whole, not the ground of it.

Schleiermacher then adds that this feeling of absolute dependence is a feeling of being related to God. "[T]his is to be understood in the sense that the Whence of our receptive and active existence, as implied in this self-consciousness, is to be designated by the word 'God,' and that this is for us the really original signification of that word."[17] Or, to use a convenient theological shorthand, the feeling of absolute dependence can be referred to as "God-consciousness." Such God-consciousness in theory accompanies every thought and every act of ours. To the extent that it does so Schleiermacher says we are "pious."

To finish our discussion of Christology, then, the feature of Jesus' personality that was so attractive and around which the Christian community formed was, Schleiermacher holds, his perfect God-consciousness. In terms of his discussion of intuition in the *Speeches*, other communities have different core intuitions that shape their experiences. The feeling of absolute dependence always exists in conjunction with concrete states of consciousness. The distinctively Christian consciousness is the consciousness of redemption though Christ. This is the root intuition around which the Christian community formed and continues to form.[18] People's experiences are accompanied to a greater or lesser extent by this God-consciousness, depending on the extent to which they cultivate this awareness, depending on their piety. But Jesus is the only human in history whose every thought, action, and experience at every stage of his human development has been accompanied by a feeling of absolute dependence, a perfect God-consciousness.

Schleiermacher's goal as a "liberal evangelical," a mediating theologian articulating Christian experience in a radically changed, modern world, is to use the language of the tradition, but to use it in ways that make sense to moderns. We saw in his young departure from the Moravian seminary that Schleiermacher struggled with the "two-natures" doctrine of Christ. This is the Christological framework, codified at the Council of Chalcedon in 451, that Jesus is one person in two natures. Like many other Christians, Schleiermacher felt that this way of talking about Jesus inevitably led to logical muddles and resulted in useless speculative controversies. B. A. Gerrish expresses the dilemma as follows:

> If Christ is one person formed out of two natures, does he also have two wills? If we answer that he has only one will, then we are forced to admit that either the divine nature or the human was incomplete, that is, lacked a will. But if we answer that he has two wills, then it seems impossible to maintain that he is one person.[19]

What is essential in the doctrine, that Schleiermacher would like to retrieve, is the experience Christians have of Christ as the mediator of a correct relationship to God. While the two-natures doctrine was infelicitously expressed, the central belief about Jesus is this: "to ascribe to Christ an absolutely powerful consciousness of God and to attribute to him an existence of God in him are entirely one and the same thing."[20]

How can we account for this perfect God-consciousness in Jesus? I think it is safe to say that this is the section of Schleiermacher's dogmatics that satisfies the fewest people. Schleiermacher writes that, because the sense of absolute dependence is a feature of human consciousness, a perfect God-consciousness is in no way unnatural. But why does it arise in this man, at this time? Here Schleiermacher says, and this is the only time he makes this move in *The Christian Faith*, that while the arising of the God-consciousness in Jesus does not violate the natural order, neither can the preceding chain of natural causes explain Jesus' God-consciousness.[21] This will satisfy neither Christians who appreciate Schleiermacher's mediating efforts to show that Christianity does not violate the natural order, nor will it satisfy Christians who prefer their theology supernatural.

I turn now to our second topic of discussion about the Introduction, the theological controversies that surround it. When first published in 1820/21, *The Christian Faith* was immediately recognized as an important and epoch-making book. Because, in part, of its radically new theological method, it was also immediately attacked and misunderstood. In preparing the second edition (published 1830/31, now the standard edition), Schleiermacher decided not to burden the book with responses to his critics. Rather, he published in 1829 two open letters to his friend G. C. Friedrich Lücke in which he discusses the criticisms.[22]

Schleiermacher says he considered reordering the major sections of the work, but decided to stick to the original outline. The order, however, did lead to some misunderstanding. Many people saw the Introduction as the most important part, and thought that the end of the book was somewhat anticlimactic. "[I]s it not true," Schleiermacher asks, "that the Introduction has been regarded as the main subject and core of the book, although it was intended only as a preliminary orientation which, strictly speaking, lies outside the discipline of dogmatics itself?"[23] For Schleiermacher, the Introduction is not part of dogmatics proper. That is, it does not begin with Christian experience, articulating it in second-order language. Rather, it "borrows propositions from Ethics" to identify what religion is as opposed to other realms of investigation, and it "borrows propositions from philosophical theology" to identify what sets Christianity off among the religions. But all of this is simply to circumscribe what it is we are talking about when we talk about Christian piety. That talk of piety comes not in the Introduction but in parts I and II. And there Schleiermacher sticks to his stated method of beginning with the specific modification of consciousness found in his religious community, as expressed in creedal statements, and attempting to articulate those experiences in a rigorous way that shows the connections that exist between the various doctrines.

If one takes the Introduction to be part of dogmatics proper, then Schleiermacher's method will fall apart. He will not be basing his theology on religious experience, but will be engaging in some kind of speculation or metaphysics that places him on the philosophical playing field.[24]

The stakes are high. Karl Barth writes,

> Is Schleiermacher's enterprise concerned (a) necessarily, intrinsically, and authentically with a Christian theology

oriented towards worship, preaching, instruction, and pastoral care? Does it only accidentally, extrinsically, and inauthentically wear the dress of a philosophy accommodated to the person of his time . . .? Or is his enterprise concerned (b) primarily, intrinsically, and authentically with a *philosophy* . . . indifferent as to Christianity and which would have wrapped itself only accidentally, extrinsically, and inauthentically in the garments of a particular theology, which here happens to be Christian?[25]

Barth, of course, takes option (b). From our own historical perspective I think a better case can be made for option (a). But my task in this chapter is not to champion but to explicate, in the hopes that theological readers will have the tools to read more, and come to their own conclusions.

Finally, in this section on the Introduction, I return to the debates in Chapter 4 about Schleiermacher's theory of religion. Above I noted that the language in the *Speeches* about sensing the infinite in the finite and the language in the Introduction about a feeling of absolute dependence amount to roughly the same thing. What causes suspicion among the nontheological readers of Schleiermacher is the next step. When Schleiermacher claims that by "God" we mean "the Whence of our receptive and active existence," it seems to Proudfoot that Schleiermacher's true colors, hidden in the *Speeches*, have been revealed. What was presented as an account of religion per se, the essence of which is a feature of our perception that gives us a sense of the whole, turns out, as we suspected all along, to be Christian apologetics. Schleiermacher from the start was talking about the Christian God.[26]

While I marked my reservations about the project of approaching religion as though it had an essence, I do not think this way of reading the *Speeches* back through the Introduction to *The Christian Faith* is quite fair. Schleiermacher is careful, more careful than many give him credit for, to distinguish his philosophical from his theological claims. In Chapter 2 we saw that he made a distinction between what we could know (this required the application of concepts, hierarchically ordered, used according to the rules of logic, and related to the order of being) and what was a matter of faith. And it was precisely the Absolute, the top of the hierarchy of concepts that was itself not a concept and so by definition could be neither thought nor known. He wrote,

> The highest would then be where the opposition of concept and object is suspended (*aufgehoben*). That would be the same that we regarded as the transcendental, the being in which the opposition of ideal and real is suspended. But this we cannot consider as knowledge. . . . It is a mere assumption (*Setzung*), that can only be compared to the totality of all combinations. (p. 172)

We cannot account for knowing without this assumption (p. 165), but we cannot think it or perceive it, "of an intuition thereof can there be absolutely no talk" (p. 164), because it is not a concept, it does not hover beneath something more general.[27]

Christians have a language for talking about this absolute, but it is the language of belief, not knowledge. Here genre becomes important. In the *Speeches* Schleiermacher addressed outsiders, literati who did not consider themselves Christian. In *The Christian Faith* he addresses theology students, already members of a particular community, already fluent users of the language and worldview that originated with Jesus. While it is true for Schleiermacher that the intuition around which every religion forms will be some version of an intuition of the infinite, Christians have a distinctive consciousness that will not be the same in every religion. Many contemporary theorists of religion will be uncomfortable with the more generic claim that all religions share the same kind of intuition, to use his early language, or that they share a feeling of absolute dependence, to use his later language. That is a discomfort I share. But it is not fair to Schleiermacher to attribute to him the more specific claim that this feeling that he holds to be universal takes the form that it takes in Christian consciousness. Schleiermacher is claiming that those formed (conceptually among other ways) by the Christian community experience this intuition as coming from God. Their conceptual apparatus that makes this experience possible is linked to Jesus' God-consciousness. Christians have a language of belief (not knowledge) with which to express this experience.

Sin and Redemption

Richard R. Niebuhr, in one of the earliest books in English that gives an essentially accurate reading of Schleiermacher's theology, claims that Schleiermacher's theology is "Christomorphic."[28] That is, the entire project is shaped by and organized around the experience of redemption related to Jesus of Nazareth. There is not room in this chapter to take up very many of the doctrines covered in Schleiermacher's systematic theology. But I do want to give an account of sin and redemption, which are central to Schleiermacher's project. We have discussed above the God-consciousness of Jesus, and we have discussed how this God-consciousness is mediated to us through the Christian community that carries within itself the picture of Jesus' personality. But what are the effects of this consciousness so mediated? What does Jesus *do* for us?[29]

Schleiermacher defines sin as follows:

> We have the consciousness of sin whenever the God-consciousness which forms part of an inner state, or is in some way added to it, determines our self-consciousness as pain; and therefore we conceive of sin as a positive antagonism of the flesh against the spirit.[30]

In other words, we have the possibility in every thought, experience, and action to accompany the thought, experience, or action with the feeling of absolute dependence, with God-consciousness. To the extent that this feeling is not present, we are in a state Schleiermacher calls "God-forgetfulness." In this state we experience, as Wyman phrases it, "a sense of incompleteness, mental discomfort, of things somehow out of joint, of the world lacking in religious meaning."[31]

Notice here that sin is not for Schleiermacher a moral problem; it is a religious problem. It is, to use a term from other theologians, a problem of alienation from God. And notice too that for Schleiermacher sin and consciousness of sin are one and the same thing. Sin has to do with how we are conscious of our relationship to the world. This is in line with Schleiermacher's theological method of a "theology of consciousness."

A couple of comments about this doctrine of sin: first, it allows Schleiermacher to jettison the traditional account of sin as a historical event resulting from the fall of Adam and Eve. Not only is that account in Genesis suspect on historical grounds, it also has conceptual problems. It cannot account for why Adam sinned (sin must have been present to cause his disobedience), and it is out of line with Schleiermacher's modern anthropology. One acts in accordance with one's nature, not on it.[32]

Second, while Schleiermacher jettisons the fall as a historical event, he is able to remain in line with two important traditional aspects of the doctrine of sin. First, he claims there is original sin. In the process of human development we think, act, and experience before we are able to develop a consciousness of the whole, a feeling of absolute dependence. So from the start our active and passive relationship to the world will not be accompanied by a God-consciousness. Second, since our actions and experience are in important ways given to us by our communities and languages (recall again the discussion of the Dialectic in Chapter 2), we will be formed by those communities' faulty God-consciousness. Schleiermacher's social account of sin is one of the great strengths of his doctrine. But what these two aspects of his doctrine of sin add up to is that every action of ours is faulty, tainted by an inadequate God-consciousness. Like Calvin, Schleiermacher holds that we are totally depraved.[33]

If we had a perfect God-consciousness, we would not avoid the pains and setbacks of human existence, but these pains would nevertheless be accompanied by the "joy" or "blessedness" of God-consciousness. Schleiermacher accounts for evil, then, as a matter of perspective. "If . . . the predominant factor is not the God-consciousness but the flesh, every impression made by the world upon us and involving an obstruction of our bodily and temporal life must be reckoned as an evil."[34] I take this to be largely in line with what Calvin says about faith:

> Now we possess a right definition of faith if we call it a firm and certain knowledge of God's benevolence toward us, founded upon the truth of the freely given promise in Christ, both revealed to our minds and sealed upon our hearts through the Holy Spirit.[35]

The redemption effected by Christ is, properly speaking, the removal of sin. When our God-consciousness is elevated by the influence of Christ's perfect God-consciousness, we have a corporate feeling of blessedness, that is, the connection of sin and evil is broken. We do not experience lack of religious meaning; pain and suffering "do not penetrate into inmost life."[36] In addition, the consciousness of deserving punishment is gone. We experience the forgiveness of sins.[37] For both Calvin and for Schleiermacher Christian faith does not mean that adversity in life ceases, but it does mean that one experiences adversity as well as good events as accompanied by consciousness of God (aware of God's benevolence, in Calvin's terms). Suffering in that case does not disturb the inner joy or blessedness of being related to God.

When teaching theology I advise my students that there is no theological model without its strong and weak suits. When one does theology systematically it quickly becomes evident that one has to choose the strong suit that seems most important, and see if one can live with the weak suits that are entailed. (You cannot have Augustine's doctrine of divine omnipotence without his doctrine of predestination, as he himself painfully came to realize over the course of his career. You cannot have Luther's justification by faith alone if you cannot put up with his low anthropology.) To put it crudely, one has to do a cost/benefit analysis of every theology under consideration. So what are the strong and weak suits of Schleiermacher's theology?

The most wholesale criticism of Schleiermacher's theology comes from Karl Barth. The core of Barth's objection to Schleiermacher is that theology must be grounded on the revealed Word of God, it cannot be grounded on the experience of the community. As World War I broke out Barth found the ties of Christian faith to German culture to be too dangerous. How can the Christian prophetically call the community to task if the Christian's faith is community-based? And indeed, it is hard to see exactly what the "picture of Christ" amounts to in some churches. In any case, as we will see in Chapter 6, Schleiermacher's theology did not prevent him from being a very active social critic and reformer.

On Schleiermacher's Christology, two perceptive criticisms were raised already in the 1830s by the theologian David Friedrich Strauss. Although Schleiermacher's move to base theology on the experience of community avoids most of the shocks delivered to other theologies by historical criticism, it is important to Schleiermacher that we see evidence in the Gospels of Jesus' perfect God-consciousness. Strauss questions whether even this much historically reliable information is available in the Gospels. Furthermore, Strauss makes a logical objection to Schleiermacher's Christology. If one is making inferences from effect back to cause, from the relatively heightened but still imperfect God-consciousness found in Christian communities back to the God-consciousness of Jesus, one is not allowed to infer a greater cause than is required to account for the effect. At most one could infer a relatively heightened God-consciousness in Jesus.

On Schleiermacher's account of sin and evil, Wyman raises at least two important questions. Is Schleiermacher's account of evil adequate? If evil is largely a matter of consciousness, does that offer the needed intellectual resources to undertake action to combat social evil, rather than merely change one's perspective about social conditions? And while Schleiermacher's theory of religion is at times pluralistic in useful ways (as we saw in the *Speeches*, the more different intuitions of the infinite in the finite the better), is not his Christology finally exclusivistic? Only Jesus' God-consciousness is perfect, and this God-consciousness is present in and mediated by the Christian community only.

Looking to the positive side of the cost/benefit ledger, Schleiermacher's theology of consciousness captures an important feature of religious experience *as* experience rather than a set of propositions about the world. He can articulate the communal nature of religious phenomena. His emphasis on Christianity as "related to the redemption accomplished by Jesus of Nazareth" stands in continuity with the central Reformation proclamation of justification by faith alone. And he can articulate this faith in such a way that it is not threatened by the sciences, natural or historical. Finally, Schleiermacher's theological method has proved enormously useful to some of the most important and world-changing theologies of the modern world. The conception of theology as an articulation of religious experience stands at the root of feminist theology, which agrees in principle and goes on to point out that women do not always have the same experience as men. This conception stands as well at the root of black theology and many of its offspring, which likewise point out that theology is based on experience, and so it is critical to articulate the experience of those traditionally excluded from the theological conversation.

CHAPTER SIX

Schleiermacher as Political Activist[1]

When I give public lectures on Schleiermacher I frequently make the claim, which I hope to have backed up sufficiently in this book on his work and influence, that Schleiermacher may be the most famous person the audience has never heard of. Once in a while someone in the audience will have heard something about Schleiermacher. When this happens the two questions I get most frequently are (1) Isn't Schleiermacher's thought too individualistic? and (2) Doesn't Schleiermacher's theology lead to quietism and disengagement? If there is such a thing, then, as the word on the street about Schleiermacher, these seem to be the two ideas about him that have trickled out of the academic guild.

It is not hard to see how a quick look at his writings might lead to these ideas. Sensing the infinite in the finite is something that happens internally, in the consciousness of an individual's perception. And Schleiermacher's most fundamental theological strategy, as we saw in the previous chapter, is to argue that the essence of religion is not a matter of thinking or doing but is properly located in the human faculty of feeling. Of those three basic human faculties most nineteenth-century thinkers agreed we all share, thinking and doing are active, feeling is passive.

I do not think either stereotype bears up under a closer look at Schleiermacher's texts. In Schleiermacher's Dialectic and Hermeneutics he has a way of accounting for the profound connection of individual and community. Each shapes the other in a way that does not shortchange the importance of either. Your experience may be individual, but the mental structures, the very concepts that make your experiences possible, are given to you by your community. In turn those structures are made up of the expressions of the individual personalities that make up the community, past and present.

If the view of Schleiermacher's thought as overly individualistic and passive does not hold up under a better reading of his corpus, that view is certainly belied by his own life. Schleiermacher was a political reformer and activist. His activities were not apart from but part of his religious view of the world. With the benefit of our historical perspective he seems to have ended up on the right side of almost every significant political battle of his day (which is another way of saying that he was one of the influential constructors of our historical perspective, an architect of the modern world).

In Chapter 1 I gave a bit of background on Schleiermacher's historical context. I want to say a little more about that here. I also mentioned what may be the most dramatic example of his activism, his role in a covert plot to overthrow the French occupiers of Prussia. I will return to that episode now that we have the intellectual background to understand the reasons for his participation. We will then look at Schleiermacher's lectures on "The Theory of the State." He lectured on this topic six times, once as a private subscription series in 1808–09, and five terms at the University of Berlin (1813, 1817, 1817–18, 1829, and 1833). Having introduced the basics of his political theory, I will show the relationship of this theory to his theology. I will then discuss a famous series of "political sermons" he preached during the French occupation, and his work as the editor of a political newspaper, *The Prussian Correspondent*. Finally, I will return to another topic of Chapter 1, Schleiermacher's important contributions to the theory of church/state relations, and his work on those relations on behalf of the Prussian Church.

Setting and Conspiracy

In the Europe into which Schleiermacher was born Germany did not exist as a political entity.[2] Rather, there were over 350 states of varying sizes and power, loosely linked by history, language, and geography. The two largest of these states were Prussia and Austria. Schleiermacher's Prussia was not a modern state but a monarchy of the ancien régime. To oversimplify things a bit, Prussians were not citizens but members of an estate (*Stand*), each subject owing specific obligations to a lord in a hierarchy of mutual obligations stretching from landless peasants up to the king. Leadership of Prussia belonged exclusively to the aristocratic estate. Kings drew on members of this estate to form their cabinets and ministries. Most importantly, in Prussia, it was this estate that provided military officers. They served the king in this capacity out of personal obligation and duty. The military troops, made up of lower estates and mercenaries, obeyed their officers, in the words of Friedrich the Great, because they were more afraid of their officers than they were of the enemy.

Schleiermacher's time was also a time of rapid change in Europe. Power and money began to shift to growing cities, and to a growing class of traders and merchants in those cities, from the landed aristocracy. One of the goals of the universities was to train men to be able to serve in government bureaucracies, regardless of the estate into which they were born. Most dramatic, of course, was the French Revolution, beginning in 1789, that eventually changed the entire political and legal shape of Europe. Schleiermacher was 20 on July 14 of that year. We saw in Chapter 1 that political differences between Schleiermacher and Count von Dohna, in whose household Schleiermacher was serving as tutor, were part of the reason Schleiermacher left that position.

Napoleon installed himself as First Consul of France in 1799, and in 1804 had himself declared emperor. Prussia did its best to remain neutral in the imperial struggles up to 1806, but Napoleon's increasing demands on Prussia finally caused King Friedrich Wilhelm III to send his famous troops out against the French. The Prussians were completely devastated by the French troops, led by Napoleon, at the battles of Jena and Auerstädt on October 14, 1806. Many Prussian troops fled the field. France took all but four

Prussian provinces for itself, and occupied those remaining four. It placed huge reparations payments on Prussia. The King and his court fled to the easternmost part of Prussia, near Königsberg. The defeat was more than a military one for Prussia. Given the role of the military in creating a large and powerful state, their disastrous performance called into question the very identity of Prussia.

On October 17, 1806, Napoleon's troops occupied Halle, where Schleiermacher was a professor. French officers were billeted in Schleiermacher's apartment. Napoleon closed down the university on October 20, and when Halle became part of the French province of Westphalia, ruled by Napoleon's brother Jerome, Schleiermacher left for Berlin.

This is the context in which Schleiermacher worked out his political philosophy. The battle that finally defeated the French in Prussia in 1813 was fought at Hallisches Tor. This is the southern gate of Berlin and the southern point of Schleiermacher's parish. It was a 10-minute walk from Trinity Church.[3] In addition to his specific efforts to defeat the French and reinvigorate Prussia, and to establish a new kind of Prussia on a constitutional model, there are three overarching goals of his to keep in mind. First, Schleiermacher endeavored to create a political model in which Prussians were citizens rather than subjects of a particular estate or lord. Schleiermacher wanted citizens who could identify with, be committed to, and work for the interests of the greater nation. Second, Schleiermacher was one of the first public intellectuals to envision and call for a greater Germany that united the loose connection of states into a single political entity. In a letter to Friedrich Schlegel in 1813 Schleiermacher writes what scholars refer to as his "political credo":

> My greatest wish after liberation, is for one true German Empire, powerfully representing the entire German folk and territory to the outside world, while internally allowing the various *Länder* and their princes a great deal of freedom to develop and rule according to their own particular needs.[4]

Third, the fact that Schleiermacher functions as a public intellectual is in itself a remarkable fact. Schleiermacher was not a member of the aristocracy. He embodied what his theory called for: citizen participation. Schleiermacher helped create, and then made use of, forums for public debate that we take for granted today but were being forged in his day. Wilhelm Dilthey writes of Schleiermacher,

> He belongs to those great men who first found a way from their private circumstances to live for the state without an official position, without ambition for political adventure, in the sure self-confidence of the citizen. Without this self-confidence life does not appear to us to be worth living any more. And yet it is not more than a half century since these men struggled and acquired it.[5]

Schleiermacher was active in a reform movement spearheaded by the King's Chief Minister, Karl Freiherr vom Stein. Stein took steps to develop a culture of citizen participation in Prussia. Schleiermacher and Stein saw lack of such participation as one of the key weaknesses that had been exposed in Prussia's defeats to the French, who fielded a citizen army. Stein began to abolish hereditary serfdom on some Prussian estates, to open the officers' corps to men from all social classes based on merit, and to create provincial legislative bodies that would begin to develop in Prussians the virtues and responsibilities of participating in governance. Stein's hope was for

> the animation of the common spirit and sense of citizenship, making use of the sleeping or misguided powers and scattered knowledge, the accord between the spirit of the nation, the reanimation of the feeling for the fatherland, independence and national honor.[6]

Schleiermacher did not join but worked with a secret society in Berlin to plan a popular uprising against the French. I briefly outlined Schleiermacher's dramatic reconnaissance mission to the King's court in Chapter 1. Schleiermacher's hope for this uprising (which did not in fact take place) was not simply to get rid of the French. He was trying to convince the King to allow Prussians to arm themselves (weapons were strictly controlled by the noble class), and he was trying to convince Prussians to play a role in their own military and political destiny. At several points Schleiermacher pushed the King hard to establish a militia (as we will see in the section below on his stint as the editor of a political newspaper).

Schleiermacher himself volunteered for duty as a military chaplain (he was not taken up on his offer) and trained with a militia (*Landsturm*) in Berlin.

Schleiermacher's goals on this trip to the Court in eastern Prussia were threefold: first, to coordinate the stashing of arms in strategic locations; second to make a plan for distributing them at the right time; and third to get permission from the Court for the secret societies to launch their uprising when they felt the time was right. Schleiermacher met with Stein, the Queen and Crown Prince, General Chief of Staff Neithardt von Gneisenau, and Minister of the War Department Gerhard von Scharnhorst. The King did not grant him a private interview but did request to hear him preach, which Schleiermacher did on September 4, 1808. The King was not supportive of attempts to conspire against the French, and the mission was largely a failure. It should be noted that when Stein's role in the conspiracy was uncovered, Napoleon forced King Wilhelm Friedrich III to replace him as Chief Minister, confiscated his estates, and placed Stein under a death sentence. As Stein fled Prussia he wrote to his wife that he gained solace by reading one of Schleiermacher's political sermons, which I discuss below.

Lectures on the State

One of the dominant theories of the state in Schleiermacher's day is one that will be familiar to contemporary Western readers, perhaps especially in the United States. It is one that Schleiermacher rejects. It is the theory that states originate with a social contract forged between rational individuals living, up to that point, in a state of nature. In exchange for giving up certain natural rights (complete freedom to do whatever I want) in order to join the state, individuals receive the benefits of state protection from internal and external threats so they can freely exercise their unalienable rights. These unalienable rights (the ones they cannot give up) are life, liberty, and pursuit of happiness.

Schleiermacher's alternate account of the origins of the state begins, not with individuals, but with households.

> [T]he state is a community, but not the original community, rather it presupposes a few already; that is a multitude of

individual humans, by which we must take notice of that which nature has set apart and bound together, and that is the two sexes. Without them there is no state because a state presupposes a succession of generations.⁷

The group, for Schleiermacher, precedes the individual.

Larger groups form over time from these households. Because of the process of mutual influence we have seen in his Dialectic and Hermeneutics, groups living in proximity with each other and interacting with each other will influence each other's language and gestures. They will form a common culture because of the link of language to reason and experience. To borrow a phrase from Durkheim, groups develop a collective conscience. When households live in proximity because they are linked genealogically Schleiermacher calls them tribes. But the same process is at work in any set of groups placed in proximity (Schleiermacher uses, for example, a hypothetical case of people thrown together by shipwreck on a desert island who over time form a group).

Over time households form larger social groups with a common language and set of customs (*Sitten*). But such a group is not yet a state. By definition a state for Schleiermacher is "the opposition of authority and subject."⁸ As we have seen, he circumscribes the phenomena he is interested in analyzing by creating a spectrum, at the top and bottom of which we find limiting cases. For states the limiting cases are anarchy and despotism. In anarchy there is no distinction of authority and subject. Nor does this distinction exist in the master-slave relationship of despotism, since the slave is not a subject. There is no reciprocity; the will is located entirely in the master. The slave is treated not as human subject but as machine.

Why would a group establish an authority, create a state? Schleiermacher holds that it is implausible that individuals form a state because they make a rational decision to give up certain natural freedoms (or rights) in return for the benefits of some enforcement of economic agreements and for mutual defense. Establishing an authority is not to facilitate working together; working together precedes the establishment of an authority. And if states were formed for mutual defense they would disband when a situation of proximate threat passed. States do make it easier to work together and they do provide defense, but neither of these activities can give rise to a state.[9]

For Schleiermacher, groups establish a state as part of their organic growth, as a means of sanctioning, expressing, and furthering their established customs and rules.

> [H]istory gives evidence that humans cannot go beyond a certain point of development without building a state. Thence it is also clear as day that progress in the pre-state condition in contrast to a situation with a state was exponentially smaller.[10]

A state is a healthy development of a social organism's development that furthers the ends of that organism and serves to express the individual personality of that organism.

If Schleiermacher has a different story to tell about the origins of the state than the dominant Enlightenment theories, he also has a different story to tell about the role of the state. For him the state is part of an organism. For Enlightenment thinkers the state is a machine, a necessary evil that is suited only to provide internal and external protection and enforce contracts. The Enlightenment view leads to the principle that "that state is best which governs least" (to quote Thomas Paine). Schleiermacher holds that the state has a more positive role to play; as the natural expression of the values and goals of a people it represents the completion of human life and the maximum of the good.[11] One of the factors that contributed to Prussia's defeat by the French, he believes, is precisely the prevalence of the Enlightenment philosophy of the state among educated and elite classes. It causes a detachment of individuals from their national community.

Links to Christology

To see how Schleiermacher's political theories are a part of his theological worldview, I want to make explicit some of the connections between his views of the state and his Christology. Recall that for Schleiermacher the essence of religion is an intuition of the infinite in the finite, and that people who have had such an intuition are driven to express it to others.

They are conscious of encompassing only a small part of it, and that which they cannot reach directly they will at least perceive through a foreign medium. Therefore he is interested in each expression of the same, and seeking to supplement himself he listens intently to every sound that he perceives of it [of such an expression].[12]

There is a social aspect to religion: people express it, and gather together to share it.
When they do gather they change each other.

So feeling . . . is not exclusively for oneself, but becomes external originally and without definite intention or reference through facial expression, gesture, tone, and indirectly through speech, and so becomes to others a revelation of the inner. This mere expression of feeling . . . passes over . . . into lively imitation, and the more the perceiver . . . is able to pass over into the same state, the more easily will this state be brought forth through the imitation.[13]

One's expressions are taken up into the gestures and speech of others, and vice versa. As we have seen in our discussions of Schleiermacher's Dialectic and Hermeneutics, this means that our possible experiences and ways of thinking, our personalities, will be shaped by those around us. When we begin to talk alike we begin to form a collective conscience, and culture, a group personality.

Jesus had a perfect God-consciousness, an unbroken awareness in everything he did and in everything that happened to him of absolute dependence. This was the feature of his personality that was expressed in his speech and gesture. It attracted others to him, and they began to imitate his speech and to gesture. In so doing the possibility of experiencing absolute dependence was opened up for them. In the collective conscience of the Christian community Jesus' personality is still present, and remains redemptive.

In discussing Schleiermacher's Christology in Chapter 5 I pointed out that this way of thinking about the ongoing presence of Christ allowed Schleiermacher to open up an alternative to the magical and empirical theologies he found inadequate. In this chapter I want to point out that all communities form the same natural, organic way, and that this has important implications for how one ought to try to organize a community. If you try to restrict the free expression of individuals in a community you disrupt the process of this mutual formation. Schleiermacher writes in the *Soliloquies*, "[E]ach should grant to the other the freedom to go where the spirit drives him or her. . . . In this way each would find in the other life and nourishment."[14] If the state imposes a-religious requirements on the church, the very possibility of the presence of Christ is under threat. Likewise for a national community. If the state tends toward the despotic end of the spectrum and citizens do not have the ability to gather together and to participate in important state decisions and actions, then the organic national spirit will not thrive but will begin to atrophy. This was precisely the flaw in Prussia's ancien régime model that was exposed in their confrontation with the French.

Political Sermons

Schleiermacher's most important contribution to the efforts to resist the French occupation came in a set of remarkable political sermons, sermons that caused Dilthey to refer to him as Germany's greatest political preacher since Luther.[15] In Chapter 5 we saw that worship services, for Schleiermacher, were the occasion for the free exchange of religious feelings. He conceived of the sermon, the highpoint of the Protestant service, as the place where the preacher presented his (only his, in Schleiermacher's day) own religious experience in such a way that the congregation could participate in and be enlivened by it. In general, Schleiermacher held it to be inappropriate to address political questions from the pulpit because (as we saw in Figure 2.2 in Chapter 2) politics are a sphere of human activity separate from religion. To preach on politics is to miss or dilute or contradict what Schleiermacher sees as the proper role of the sermon.

But Schleiermacher also held that in unusual circumstances, if the community was deeply affected by political events, the preacher could not ignore them. The worshipers would not find the peace they sought, piety could not be elevated, because the exchange of religious feelings could not occur if such unusual events were ignored. Napoleon's invasion was such an event. Schleiermacher begins a sermon on March 28, 1813: "[T]hrough an unusual occurrence we find our series of talks on the suffering redeemer interrupted, and our gathering today dedicated to a completely different subject. How we all were moved to the core through the events of last week!"[16]

Napoleon censored the press and public assemblies were banned. Contemporaries of Schleiermacher's report that his political sermons played a huge role in reinvigorating the Berlin populace and framing the events of the day. I want to look at three of these sermons that present, in popular form, some of the most important views that Schleiermacher makes in his lectures on the state. In these sermons Schleiermacher makes the case that (1) there is a close link between individual and community characteristics; (2) states are organic expressions of these cultural traits, and full development of each individual depends on participating fully in such a state; and (3) the healthiest form of state is one that breaks down inherited status, instead allowing individuals to develop freely, then drawing on the strength of those individuals. In making these three points he ties them to his theological worldview.

On November 23, 1806 Schleiermacher preached a sermon in Halle with the title, "On Making Use of Public Disasters." This is about five weeks after the defeat at Jena and Auerstädt and the occupation of Halle by French troops. Schleiermacher had not yet relocated to Berlin. Here we see Schleiermacher's arguments, with which we are familiar from his Dialectic, Hermeneutics, and Christology, that individuals and groups mutually form each other. "Many say, it is not my mistake [referring to Jena and Auerstädt], but the generals', or the soldiers', or those who hold the reigns of power. This is to make a new mistake, to make a sharp distinction between the individual and the whole." Leaders and people have the same characteristics:

> Where fearlessness and contempt for danger, love of order and faithful obedience are the character of the members of a people, there lack of courage and independence cannot reveal themselves in great quantities, when only through the former virtues can the community be saved.

"The whole and the part had one life, one destiny—also the same virtue and ethos."[17]

Schleiermacher argues against the Enlightenment position that the goal of human development is to be a cosmopolitan, or a "world citizen," and for the position that humans are at their best when they are fully committed to the community of which they are a part, in a sermon titled, "How Greatly the Dignity of a Person is Enhanced when One Adheres with All One's Soul to the Civil Union to Which One Belongs" (preached August 24, 1806, two months before Jena and Auerstädt). Schleiermacher thinks he has scriptural warrant for his position. His text is Ephesians 2.19: "You are no longer guests or aliens, but citizens with the holy and God's fellow tenant."[18] Schleiermacher warns against the view that the state is an artificial machine. This view leads to a lack of public spirit, "in which there is no lively care for public affairs, no eager taking part in the destiny of the community." States are not created out of need for defense—"It is not need that binds men but an inner air and love, a given common existence, an indestructible common voice." Paul's use of the metaphor of citizenship to describe faith indicates Paul's high regard for citizenship.

Schleiermacher argues that when a state is founded, "it is one of the greatest steps forward possible for our race." Individualists are limited, in what they can achieve, to the accomplishments of an individual. Great achievements require common effort. "Everything great requires a great mass of powers, which humans have only in connection with one another." If we recall Schleiermacher's Philosophical Ethics, in which he argued that humans are the organ of the increasing interpenetrating of reason and nature, which is the goal of history, we can see why Schleiermacher concludes that "[t]hese associations belong to the house of God. It follows that patriotism is good, and those who think it is not for them are like guests or aliens."[19]

Schleiermacher links his view of what makes for a healthy community, the view that is presupposed in his Christology, with the reform project of Stein and others in a sermon in Berlin on January 24, 1808: "On Proper Respect for Greatness from an Earlier Time." The occasion was the birthday of Friedrich the Great. A conservative faction in Prussia had argued that Prussia became weak and vulnerable to the French because it had moved away from the traditional social arrangements in Friedrich's day. "Others wish, if not for Friedrich, then to return to the external arrangements and the whole state of an earlier gleaming time, in the belief that in these lived the happy and elevating power."

But Schleiermacher holds that Friedrich's greatness was based (in addition to his natural talent) on Friedrich's willingness to begin to break down sharp distinctions of rank. People won respect "through their mental gifts and ways of thinking." "[D]o not forget that it was a fundamental law of the government of that great king that all citizens were equal before the law." Friedrich extended freedom of faith to his subjects because he wanted subjects worthy of being ruled.

Schleiermacher's text for this sermon is Mathew 24.1–2, in which Jesus prophesies the destruction of the Temple. The Temple was a symbol of the Jews' greatness—what lesson do we learn from its destruction? Schleiermacher argues that the Jews were wise to hope, not for the return of David, but for someone from David's line—a messiah who does not bring back the past but embodies the spirit that made the past great.[20]

It is precisely the freedom to develop as individuals that makes a nation great, as it is the common spirit of that nation that makes individuals great. The lesson of the French occupation is that Prussia, holding on to its traditional social arrangements, had been defeated by a modern nation with new social arrangements, a citizen army of committed French citizens versus a traditional model of nobles, serfs, and mercenaries. Schleiermacher's political sermons are an effort in pastoral care during troubled times, an effort to interpret current events through a theological lens, and an effort to transform the way his congregation thought about themselves and their community in the hopes that, at the end of the war, a new kind of community would emerge.

The Prussian Correspondent

One of the least known activities of Schleiermacher was his role as editor of *The Prussian Correspondent* (*Der preussische Correspondent*) from July 1, 1813 to September 30, 1813. *The Prussian Correspondent* was one of a new breed of newspapers in Germany that gathered reports from travelers and officials and presented them to a reading public interested in political issues.

The very idea of such a paper speaks to the project of developing an informed and involved citizenry.[21]

Much of what is published in *The Prussian Correspondent* is not authored by Schleiermacher. But by analyzing dominant themes one can discern the editorial priorities he brought to the paper.[22] The subject to which Schleiermacher devotes the most attention are the creation of a militia and a reserve army. We saw above that one of Schleiermacher's goals in the conspiracy to overthrow the French was to change the political culture of Prussia and to have Prussians take responsibility for and participate in their own defense. The issue of who has rights to own which weapons was a hot one in Prussia as in many places of the ancient régime—nobles closely guarded their privileges. Schleiermacher and the reformers pushed hard for the King to form militias and reserves, but the King, wary of changing traditional roles for the military and traditional rights surrounding weapons, waffled.

Events of 1813 largely took this decision out of the King's hands. When the tide turned against Napoleon and various European nations began to form alliances to counterattack, Prussia was in need of troops. On March 17 the King issued the address "To My People" ("An Mein Volk"), calling for a militia. In April he formed a reserve army.

One of Schleiermacher's activities as editor had long-lasting effects on his life and career. This was an article Schleiermacher wrote on July 14, 1813. In June of that year Prussia and its allies agreed to an armistice (at least temporary) with France. All the reformers were highly critical of the armistice. They felt it continued the pattern of wavering of King Wilhelm Friedrich III, that it would allow the French to regroup, and that the war had to be carried through to its conclusion in order to achieve the kind of transformation they had in mind for Prussia's political culture. On June 11 the King ordered his censors to keep the Berlin newspaper editors on a very short leash. On July 14 Schleiermacher wrote that while some "want to recover from their exhaustion," others "believe that from the results of the war to this point no peace is to be expected . . . and that if such a peace could be concluded between individual powers, Germany in general and our state in particular require an enormous development of strength, as is only possible under exertions of war, to arrive at a worthy state out of which health and well-being could develop."

The King read this as, at best, a criticism of his government as weak, and at worst a call for a violent change of government. He ordered the Interior Minister to fire Schleiermacher from his state positions (pastor, professor) and to banish him from Prussia. Karl von Hardenberg, Stein's replacement as Chief Minister, watered down the language before sending the order to Interior Minister Kaspar Friedrich von Schuckman. He in turn interpreted the order as a warning to Schleiermacher to tread more carefully or be faced with these consequences. Schleiermacher was investigated for high treason in October 1813, but the investigation went nowhere. He turned over the editorship of *The Prussian Correspondent* to Achim von Arnim on October 1, 1813.

Church/State Relations

In Chapter 1 I mentioned that Schleiermacher's first university position came about in part because of an essay he wrote in 1804 calling for the unification of the Reformed and Lutheran confessions in Prussia. King Friedrich Wilhelm III also wanted to unify the confessions, and so he made an effort to create a position for the young Schleiermacher in Halle to keep him at Prussian institution.

Plans for unification were largely put on hold during the Wars of Liberation (as the anti-Napoleon campaigns were called in Prussia), but in 1814 the King again took up the cause, establishing a commission on September 17 to look into the possibility of unification. Schleiermacher remained a firm supporter of unification, but his efforts in the reform movement, and in particular his editorship of *The Prussian Correspondent*, had soured his relationship with the King. Looking at Schleiermacher's criticisms of the King's efforts at unification, and how Schleiermacher thought it ought to be undertaken, will reveal a lot about how Schleiermacher conceived the proper relationship of church and state.

The King's commission saw their job as one of liturgy reform. Schleiermacher attacked the commission for putting the cart before the horse. Given Schleiermacher's views on the role of worship as the free circulation of religious feelings, we can understand his view that reform should come not from the top down but from an inner impulse of the community. The commission "came together not of itself, by virtue of a divine inner call," "rather [it] was sought after and established by an authority which, though universally honored and also recognized for its pious views [he means the King], is nevertheless worldly."[23] It does not belong to civil authorities to take charge of ecclesiastical changes. One thing to note here is the architectonic shift to a modern-world division of labor and away from ancien régime social arrangements. Referring back to the boxes of separate human activities from Schleiermacher's Ethics in Figure 2.2 in Chapter 2, we see Schleiermacher establishing definitions and roles for religion and for government that Westerners now take for granted. These definitions and roles are a major shift from arrangements of the social world into which Schleiermacher was born, a world in which a paternalistic monarch is indeed responsible for the religious lives of his subjects.

Unsurprisingly, given Schleiermacher's view of who should take the leading role in church reforms, he believed that the proper form of church government was a synod (the Presbyterian model) that included freely elected representatives, both lay and clergy, and from both Lutheran and Reformed congregations. Further, he held that the church needed a constitution that protected it from meddling by the secular government. Also unsurprisingly, in the reactionary environment that followed Napoleon's defeat, synods smacked too much of popular legislative bodies. The King had ordered on April 30, 1815 that churches in Prussian territories should be governed by consistories.

On October 30, 1817, the Berlin churches did celebrate the 300th anniversary of the Reformation with a joint celebration of the Lord's Supper. Schleiermacher, with his Lutheran friend and colleague Philipp Marheineke, officiated in the Nicolai church, with the King in attendance. The celebration, of course, did not solve the political or structural issues of church reform.

The final chapter in the struggle of Schleiermacher with the king on church/state relationships began in 1821. The King desired a liturgical renewal and was dismayed at the large variations in liturgies used in churches throughout Prussia. He created his own order of worship (assisted by Job von Witzleben), and attempted to impose it on the church.

Schleiermacher attacked. He argued that the order of worship should be determined by the congregation, not by external civil authorities. He also argued that to impose it in the face of resistance was oppressive. "For when a significant part of the clergy must be dismissed to put a liturgy into motion (of which there are examples), then that is already the oppression of the whole church."[24] Kurt Nowak writes, "That was bold. Such a manner of expression could only be used by a man who in the fight over the sovereignty of the liturgy was also leading a fight for the political rights of Christians and citizens."[25]

The King personally took up the pen to respond in 1827 (the essay is coauthored by Neander). The King appeals to Luther's authority as the force for liturgical renewal (his liturgy had been closely modeled on Luther's). Schleiermacher's response mocks the new liturgy as a "[c]omposition of a roll of the dice."[26] He argued that Luther's liturgy was still heavily influenced by Catholicism, and he pointed out the irony of basing a Reformed renewal on an appeal to the authority of tradition. It is in his essay that Schleiermacher's famous phrase appears: "The Reformation still goes on!"[27]

In the end the King simply ordered the adoption of the new liturgy. He allowed for a few regional variations, and he allowed Schleiermacher personally some leeway. Schleiermacher was allowed to face the congregation rather than the altar while praying; he was freed from the requirement to make the sign of the cross; and he was freed from having to recite the Apostles' Creed. Near the end of Schleiermacher's life there was a mild reconciliation with the King, who in July 1830 awarded him the order of the Red Eagle (third class).

I have tried in this chapter to accomplish three things. First, to describe the wide range of political activities Schleiermacher was engaged in. At least in the case of its author, Schleiermacher's theology did not lead to passivism or quietism. Second, I have tried to show the basis of Schleiermacher's political philosophy, which is rooted in his expressivist anthropology and his view of the role of human activity as the organ of reason in the unfolding ethical progress of history. Finally, I have sought to show how Schleiermacher's political thought and activity is shaped by his theological views. The story of secularization in the modern world is complicated and contested, but there is clearly no easy replacement of religious commitment with national commitment. For Schleiermacher the second is caused by the first.

Conclusion

In Chapter 1, I connected Schleiermacher's impressively wide intellectual interests to the context of his particular time and place. In subsequent chapters I have tried to introduce readers in an accessible but sophisticated way to some of the most important contributions rising from his intellectual interests. Chapter 2 focused on his epistemology and philosophy of history, locating them in the generation of post-Kantian thinkers sometimes given the label "counter-Enlightenment." In his focus on language, and in his architectonic of the various disciplines of human thought and various fields of human endeavor, Schleiermacher plays a significant role in the development in Western culture that Isaiah Berlin calls "the greatest single shift in the consciousness of the West that has occurred." The importance of language is emphasized again in Chapter 3 on hermeneutics. Here we see Schleiermacher's argument that hermeneutics, while necessary for interpretation of the Bible and ancient texts, is also a necessarily human activity. We live in sea of language, our lives a constant process of interpretation and translation.

Chapter 4 turns to the use made of Schleiermacher in the contemporary field of religious studies. Here he has functioned as a bête noire for a certain theoretical tradition that would like to move the study of religion away from the humanities and toward the social sciences and "hard" sciences. Lost in this discussion of Schleiermacher as theorist of religion is what Schleiermacher himself had to say about religion. I have tried to clear away some of the long reception history of misreadings in English, give a full and accurate description of Schleiermacher on religion, and assess the ways in which I find his theoretical commitments to be helpful and the ways I find them to be flawed.

CONCLUSION

Chapter 5 turns to Schleiermacher's theology proper. I focused on his Christology, and his doctrines of sin and redemption. I also tried to give a fair assessment of the role the Introduction plays in his classic systematic theology, *The Christian Faith*. Having made available a rich understanding of his Ethics, Dialectic, and Hermeneutics, I hope to have been able to show some of the strengths of his theology, and clear away some of the typical misunderstandings of it. Chapter 6 looked at Schleiermacher's role as a German activist and public intellectual, theorizing a modern unified nation-state, and its proper relationship to the church.

The reading I give of various parts of his body of work is not uncontroversial. One goal of a book like this is to take my best shot at articulating clearly the best reading possible given the current rapidly improving state of texts available. I do not pretend to have given the definitive reading, but in staking a place in the controversies I do hope to stick my neck out far enough that I can fruitfully continue to talk and argue with other readers of Schleiermacher. These discussions so far have been the most illuminating and enjoyable of my professional life. Throughout I hope I have been able to make his own texts accessible, and compelling enough that readers will want to turn from this book to his writings. If I have been able to do this to some extent I will count this book a success.

NOTES

Chapter One

1 Cited by Kurt Nowak, *Schleiermacher: Leben, Werk und Wirkung* (Göttingen: Vandenhoeck & Ruprecht, 2001), p. 7. There are a number of good biographies of Schleiermacher. Nowak's is the definitive one. In English the most complete biography is a translation of Martin Redeker's *Friedrich Schleiermacher: Leben und Werk* (Berlin: deGruyter, 1968), English: *Schleiermacher: Life and Thought* (trans. John Wallhausser; Philadelphia: Fortress Press, 1973). Perhaps the best concise introduction to Schleiermacher's theology is B. A. Gerrish's *A Prince of the Church: Schleiermacher and the Beginnings of Modern Theology* (Philadelphia: Fortress Press, 1984). Terrence N. Tice artfully connects Schleiermacher's biography with his thought in *Schleiermacher* Abingdon Pillars of Theology (Nashville: Abingdon Press, 2006). The introduction and first two chapters of James M. Brandt's *All Things New: Reform of Church and Society in Schleiermacher's Christian Ethics* Columbia Series in Reformed Theology (Louisville: Westminster John Knox Press, 2001) give an insightful biographical account. Still useful is Wilhelm Dilthey's *Leben Schleiermachers* (first published in Berlin by G. Reimer in 1870). Dilthey had access to several manuscripts that are not available to later biographers, and his biography is both insightful and an important milestone in the history of modern biography. One must use it with care, since at key points some of Dilthey's interpretations are more in line with Dilthey's own thought than with Schleiermacher's. He also gets some details of Schleiermacher's employment at the Charité Hospital wrong. I have made use of all these resources in preparing this chapter. Here I cite only direct quotes, or note when I follow a particular author's interpretation of the significance of events. Translations in this chapter and this book are mine unless otherwise noted. When available I cite German originals followed by the best available English translation.

2 See James J. Sheehan, *German History 1770–1866* (Oxford: Oxford University Press, 1989), p. 58.

3 Immanuel Kant, *Foundations of the Metaphysics of Morals and What Is Enlightenment?* (Library of Liberal Arts; trans. Lewis White Beck; Upper Saddle River, NJ: Prentice Hall, 1995), p. 88.

4 Friedrich Schleiermacher, the first, 1799 edition of *On Religion: Speeches to Its Cultured Despisers* (Cambridge Texts in the History of Philosophy; ed. and trans. Richard Crouter; Cambridge: Cambridge University Press, 1988), p. 8.

5 I follow here the outline of the story, and I quote the correspondence as translated by Gerrish, *A Prince of the Church*, pp. 25–26.

6 Gerrish, *A Prince of the Church*, p. 26.

7 A full treatment of the influence of Spinoza on Schleiermacher can be found in Julia A. Lamm, *The Living God: Schleiermacher's Theological Appropriation of Spinoza* (University Park: Pennsylvania State University Press, 1996).

8 Cited in Nowak, *Schleiermacher*, p. 73.

9 These characterizations are cited in Brandt, *All Things New*, p. 3.

10 Cited in Nowak, *Schleiermacher*, p. 81.

11 Cited in Nowak, *Schleiermacher*, p. 83.

12 Cited in Nowak, *Schleiermacher*, p. 88.

13 Schleiermacher, *Speeches*, p. 24.

14 Also dating to this period in his life is Schleiermacher's important *Monologen (Soliloquies)*, 1800.

15 I follow here Brandt, *All Things New*, p. 33.

16 Here I follow Nowak, *Schleiermacher*, pp. 141 and 256–71.

17 Schleiermacher also wrote during his time in Stolp "Outline of a Criticism of Theories of Ethics to This Time."

18 Schleiermacher's lecture notes, as well as notes taken by students in his lectures on church history, have been published in the *Kritische Gesamtausgabe* II.6 (ed. Simon Gerber; Berlin: de Gruyter, 2006). When I cite the *Kritische Gesamtausgabe*, I abbreviate the title as *KGA* in all but the first citation for each work.

19 *Aus Schleiermacher's Leben. In Briefen* (Band 2; Berlin: G. Reimer, 1861), p. 106.

20 A good collection of essays on Schleiermacher and the importance of the founding of the University of Berlin has been edited by Albert Blackwell with Edwina Lawler, *Friedrich Schleiermacher and the*

Founding of the University of Berlin: The Study of Religion As a Scientific Discipline (Lewiston: Edwin Mellen Press, 1991).

21 This sermon has been translated by Albert Blackwell and is reprinted in Friedrich Schleiermacher, *Servant of the Word: Selected Sermons of Friedrich Schleiermacher* (ed. and trans. Dawn DeVries; Philadelphia: Fortress Press, 1987). One could introduce Schleiermacher to undergraduates most accessibly with this sermon, the *Christmas Eve Dialogue*, and his sermon "The Power of Prayer in Relation to Outward Circumstances," translated by Mary Wilson in a republished collection titled *Selected Sermons of Friedrich Schleiermacher* (Eugene: Wipf & Stock, n.d.).

22 English-speaking scholars disagree on whether to translate the title of *Der christliche Glaube* as *The Christian Faith* or *Christian Faith*. The most literal translation is *The Christian Faith*. But there are times when German demands the article and English does not. The article carries connotations in English that it does not in German. Schleiermacher values diversity of religious experience, and therefore diversity of theology. He offers a description of the faith of one particular Christian community, not the only true expression of the faith of all Christians. I have kept with the most common practice of using the article (the only existing full English translation of *Der christliche Glaube* uses it, though there is a forthcoming translation that does not). This is the practice that usually sounds like the best stylistic choice to my ear.

23 Letter from Reimer, cited in R. C. Raack, "A New Schleiermacher Letter on the Conspiracy of 1808," *Zeitschrift für Religions- und Geistesgeschichte* 16 (1964), pp. 209–23.

24 See Hajo Holbern, *A History of Modern Germany 1648–1840* (New York: Alfred A. Knopf, 1961), p. 467.

25 Schleiermacher's writings on church politics have been published as volume I.9 of the *Kritische Gesamtausgabe* (Berlin: de Gruyter, 2000). Many of the relevant materials on this topic have been translated by Iain G. Nicol in *Friedrich Schleiermacher on Creeds, Confessions and Church Union: That They May Be One* (Lewiston: Edwin Mellen, 2004). The phrase "[t]he Reformation still goes on!" is from Schleiermacher's essay, "Gespräch zweier selbst überlegender evangelischer Christen über die Schrift: Luther in Bezug auf die neue preussische Agende. Ein letztes Wort oder ein erstes" ["Conversation of Two Self-Reflective Evangelical Christians on the Book: Luther in Relation to the New Prussian Church Service. A Final Word or a First One," *Kritische Gesamtausgabe* I.9 (ed. Günter Meckenstock with Hans-Friedrich Traulsen; Berlin: de Gruyter, 2000), p. 471.

Chapter Two

1 Taylor is primarily concerned with the issues confronting Hegel, but we can see many of the leading lights of this generation: Schleiermacher, Herder, Fichte, Schelling, the Humbolts, the Schlegels, Novalis, and on and on, wrestling with the same problems.
2 Cited and translated by Paul Guyer and Allen Wood in the "Introduction to the *Critique of Pure Reason*," The Cambridge Edition of the Works of Immanuel Kant (Cambridge: Cambridge University Press, 1998), p. 1.
3 Kant, *Prolegomena to Any Future Metaphysics with Selections from the Critique of Pure Reason* (Cambridge Texts in the History of Philosophy rev. edn; ed. and trans. Gary Hatfield; Cambridge: Cambridge University Press, 2004), p. 10.
4 David Hume, *An Enquiry Concerning Human Understanding* and *A Letter from a Gentleman to His Friend in Edinburgh* (ed. Eric Steinberg; Indianapolis: Hackett, 1977), p. 28.
5 Kant, *Prolegomena*, p. 12.
6 Kant, *Prolegomena*, p. 7.
7 Kant, *Prolegomena*, p. 10.
8 Kant, *Prolegomena*, p. 33.
9 Kant, *Prolegomena*, p. 34 (emphasis in original).
10 These definitions are from the online version of the *New Oxford American Dictionary*, accessed June 21, 2012.
11 Kant, *Critique of Pure Reason* (236/A114) (Cambridge Edition of the Works of Immanuel Kant; ed. and trans. Paul Guyer and Allen W. Wood; Cambridge: Cambridge University Press, 1998).
12 *Critique of Pure Reason* (A15/B29), p. 135.
13 Kant, *Critique of Pure Reason* (A51/B75), pp. 193–94.
14 Charles Taylor, *Hegel* (Cambridge: Cambridge University Press, 1975), p. 23.
15 Taylor, *Hegel*, p. 24.
16 Taylor, *Hegel*, p. 24.
17 Taylor, *Hegel*, pp. 24–25.
18 Taylor, *Hegel*, pp. 27–28.
19 Schleiermacher never prepared a manuscript of his Dialectic for publication. The texts we have consist of notes he prepared for

his lecture courses at the University of Berlin, and notes taken by students attending those lectures. David Friedrich Strauss, who attended some of Schleiermacher's lectures, compared taking notes of Schleiermacher's lectures to trying to photograph a dancer in full motion. Schleiermacher's goal in lecturing was not to present a finished product; rather, it was to think through an issue and allow his listeners to enter into the thinking process with him. His own notes are intended merely as memory prompts of ideas to think about. When discussing Schleiermacher's lectures I quote mostly from an anonymous set of student notes from the 1818/1819 lectures, recently found in an attic. This manuscript, consisting of 796 pages carefully written out with few abbreviations, is the fullest account of the lectures we have. I have checked these notes with the notes Schleiermacher used in presenting these lectures. Andreas Arndt, in his introduction to the critical edition of the *Lectures on Dialectic*, notes their "special quality." See his "Editorische Bericht," in Friedrich Daniel Ernst Schleiermacher, *Vorlesungen über die Dialektik*. I have heard scholars refer to them as "ein Wunder." *Kritische Gesamtausgabe* [KGA] 10, pp. 1–2 (Berlin: de Gruyter, 2002), p. LXXI. Parenthetical references to the *Dialectic* in this section are to page numbers in 1818/1819 anonymous notes in the *KGA* 10, p. 2. Translations are mine.

20 Kant provides an analogous architectonic of knowledge in the Preface to the *Foundations of the Metaphysics of Morals* (trans. Lewis White Beck; Upper Saddle River, NJ: Prentice Hall, 2nd edn, 1995), pp. 3–8.

21 Friedrich Schleiermacher, *Lectures on Philosophical Ethics* (Cambridge Texts in the History of Philosophy; ed. Robert B. Louden; trans. Louise Adey Huish; Cambridge: Cambridge University Press, 2002), p. 5.

22 In this discussion of Schleiermacher's architectonic of knowledge I follow James Brandt, *All Things New*, pp. 67–70. The chart is reproduced from p. 69. It is in turn a modification of a chart distributed in a graduate seminar by B. A. Gerrish at the University of Chicago Divinity School, Spring 1982.

23 Kant, *Critique of Pure Reason* (A61/B85), p. 198.

24 Note that Kant makes an analogous move, as part of his moral theory rather than his epistemology. Whereas Schleiermacher thinks that our cognition requires that we posit (but know nothing about) an all encompassing absolute, Kant argues that we cannot know God but must assume God as a regulative principle that makes sense of our moral lives.

25 Kant says something analogous when he agrees with the nominal definition of truth as "the agreement of cognition with its object" (A58/B82, p. 197). But recall that by "object" Kant insists always on our representation, and never refers to the thing-in-itself. And Kant argues in his Third Critique that in the experience of beauty we get hints that nature (or being in Schleiermacher's terms) is in fact in accord with our thinking. But these hints come at the back end, so to speak, of Kant's account, not as an assumption at the front end that we need to account for knowing.

26 Kant, *Critique of Pure Reason* (A87/B119), p. 221.

27 Schleiermacher, "Aufzeichnung zum Kolleg 1811," *Kritische Gesamtausgabe* II.10, 1 *Vorlesungen über die Dialektik* (ed. Andreas Arndt; Berlin: Walter de Gruyter 2002), p. 58. Terrence N. Tice has translated these 1811 lecture notes. This is the only version of the *Dialectic* available in English. See *Dialectic or, The Art of Doing Philosophy: A Study Edition of the of the 1811 Notes* (Oxford: Oxford University Press, 2000).

28 The sense in which Schleiermacher claims to know more than Kant, as I also write above, is that our concepts do correspond more or less to beings. So while we never have direct, unmediated, preconceptual knowledge of things-in-themselves, we do over the course of human history and the scientific process begin to approach knowledge of them asymptotically. On this account knowledge, for Schleiermacher, would be along the same lines of the "virtually unconditioned" as described by Bernard Lonergan. We move from prospective judgment to the virtually unconditioned when we have accounted for the conditions that would cause us to make a "reasonable pronouncement," and fulfilled those conditions. We have answered the pertinent questions of which we are aware. We then can say we know something. Lonergan's account (this is the force of the "virtual") does not preclude the possibility of further relevant questions we had not considered in the future. See Bernard Lonergan, *Insight: A Study of Human Understanding* (Toronto: University of Toronto Press, 5th edn, 1992), chapter 10, esp. p. 305.

29 For good current work in English on Schleiermacher's Ethics (in the narrower sense the term is more commonly used) see Brent W. Sockness, "Schleiermacher and the Ethics of Authenticity: The Monologen of 1800," *Journal of Religious Ethics* 32/3 (Winter 2004), pp. 477–517 and "The Forgotten Moralist: Friedrich Schleiermacher and the Science of Spirit," *Harvard Theological Review* 96/3 (July 2003), pp. 317–48. See also Jacqueline

Mariña, *Transformation of the Self in the Thought of Friedrich Schleiermacher* (Oxford: Oxford University Press, 2008).
30 Schleiermacher, *Ethics*, p. 8.
31 Schleiermacher, *Ethics*, p. 9.
32 Schleiermacher, *Ethics*, pp. 6–7.
33 Schleiermacher, *Ethics*, p. 10.
34 Schleiermacher, *Ethics*, p. 14.
35 Schleiermacher, *Ethics*, p. 14.
36 This helpful language was suggested to me by Dave Scott.
37 See Kant's "On the Use of Teleological Principles in Philosophy (1788)," in *Race* (trans. John Mark Mikkelsen; ed. Robert Bernasconi; Oxford: Blackwell, 2001), pp. 37–56.

Chapter Three

1 Michael Forster identifies three stages in Schleiermacher's thought on the relationship of thought to language: an early "crude" phase in which the two are identified, a "slightly better" equation of thought with inner language, and a later "more defensible" position in which thought is bound to and dependent on language but not equated with language. See Michael N. Forster, "Herder's Philosophy of Language, Interpretation, and Translation: Three Fundamental Principles," *The Review of Metaphysics* 56 (December 2002), p. 330 note 23.

2 The term is coined by Berlin, who calls it the "expressionist" self. Taylor largely follows Berlin in his analysis of the key features of this anthropology, and in his discussion of some of the central figures, who belong to the generation described in Chapter 2 as struggling with the legacy of Kant. Taylor alters the name to "expressivist" to avoid any possible confusion with the nineteenth-century movement in art called Expressionist.

3 Paul Ricoeur, "Schleiermacher's Hermeneutics," *The Monist* 60/2 (April 1977), pp. 181–97. As Wolfgang Hübener notes, it does not detract from Schleiermacher's achievement to recognize that he does not create modern hermeneutics ex nihilo, as some of his champions (most notably Dilthey) have indicated. See Wolfgang Hübener, "Schleiermacher und die hermeneutische Tradition," in *Internationaler Schleiermacher-Kongress* (ed. Ebeling Birkner and Selge Kimmerle; Berlin: de Gruyter, 1985), pp. 561–74.

4 "Speech is admittedly also mediation of thought for the individual. Thought is prepared by inner discourse, and to this extent discourse is only the thought itself which has come into existence." Friedrich Schleiermacher, *Hermeneutik und Kritik* (ed. with an introduction by Manfred Frank; Frankfurt am Main: Suhrkamp, 1977), pp. 76–7. *Hermeneutik und Kritik* was originally edited by Friedrich Lücke on the basis of Schleiermacher's handwritten notes and several sets of student lecture notes, and published as Section I, Volume 7 of *Friedrich Schleiermacher's sämmtliche Werke* (Berlin: G. Reimer, 1838). I cite *Hermeneutics and Criticism* by page number in Frank's edition, and in the English translation, *Hermeneutics and Criticism and Other Writings* (trans. and ed. Andrew Bowie; Cambridge: Cambridge University Press, 1998). Quotations from *Hermeneutics and Criticism* are Bowie's translation, which I have checked against the original.

5 Throughout this chapter I will use "speech act" as a short hand for any human product of language, written or oral. The term is not perfect as it tends to slight the written, on the one hand, and the nonverbal, on the other, but listing all these possibilities at each mention is unwieldy. For Schleiermacher, interpretation includes a very wide range of behaviors, including not only written and spoken words but gestures, facial expressions, artistic productions, "body language," and so on.

6 I write "something like" because there are special cases in which the interpreter can know better than the speaker himself or herself what he or she intended to say.

7 Schleiermacher, *Hermeneutics and Criticism*, pp. 102–03/31–32.

8 Schleiermacher, *Hermeneutics and Criticism*, pp. 168/91.

9 This is Schleiermacher's definition of art.

10 In this, Jack Forstman has argued, Schleiermacher is closely related to Friedrich Schlegel's early view of irony. See Jack Forstman, *A Romantic Triangle: Schleiermacher and Early German Romanticism* (Missoula: Scholars Press, 1977), p. 103; and "The Understanding of Language by Friedrich Schlegel and Schleiermacher," *Soundings* 51 (1968), pp. 146–65.

11 Richard E. Palmer, *Hermeneutics: Interpretation Theory in Schleiermacher, Dilthey, Heidegger, and Gadamer* (Evanston: Northwestern University Press, 1969).

12 Hans-Georg Gadamer, *Truth and Method* (ed. Joel C. Weinsheimer and Donald G. Marshall; Continuum, 2nd rev. edn, 1993); Cornel West, "Schleiermacher's Hermeneutics and the Myth of the Given," *Union Seminary Quarterly Review* 34 (1979), pp. 71–84.

13 Heinz Kimmerle tries to defend Schleiermacher against Gadamer's charge of overstressing psychology by arguing that the early Schleiermacher emphasizes the grammatical task appropriately, but the later Schleiermacher does tend to stress the technical side too much. See Heinz Kimmerle, "Forward to the German Edition," and "Editor's Introduction," in F. D. E. Schleiermacher, *Hermeneutics: The Handwritten Manuscripts* (ed. Kimmerle; trans. James Duke and Jack Forstman; Atlanta: Scholars Press, 1977). Kimmerle places the blame for the view that Schleiermacher overpsychologizes on Lücke, who redacted the first published manuscript of Hermeneutics, and on Dilthey, who found in this version the roots of his theory of understanding as psychological reconstruction (for Dilthey this method of understanding is the appropriate one for the humanities; explanation is the appropriate method for the natural sciences). Kimmerle's edition of the Hermeneutics is an attempt to give a more balanced version of Schleiermacher by making available earlier texts.

14 Schleiermacher, *Hermeneutics and Criticism*, pp. 167/90.

15 Schleiermacher, *Hermeneutics and Criticism*, pp. 169/92–93. Emphasis added.

16 Palmer, *Hermeneutics*, pp. 87 and 90.

17 Bruce D. Marshall, "Hermeneutics and Dogmatics in Schleiermacher's Theology," *The Journal of Religion* 67 (January 1987), p. 18.

18 See Wolfgang Virmond, "Neue Textgrundlagungen zu Schleiermacher's früher Hermeneutik: Prolegomena zur kritischen Edition," in *Internationaler Schleiermacher-Kongress* (ed. Ebeling Birkner and Selge Kimmerle; Berlin: de Gruyter, 1985), pp. 575–90.

19 Schleiermacher, *Hermeneutics and Criticism*, pp. 170/93.

20 Both Palmer and Marshall omit this important qualifier.

21 Schleiermacher, *Hermeneutics and Criticism*, pp. 178/101–02.

22 Schleiermacher, *Hermeneutics and Criticism*, pp. 179–80/102–03.

23 Hans-Georg Gadamer, "The Problem of Language in Schleiermacher's Hermeneutics," in *Schleiermacher as Contemporary* (ed. Robert Funk; New York: Herder and Herder, 1970), p. 75.

24 Gadamer, "The Problem of Language," p. 77.

25 Ricoeur, "Schleiermacher's Hermeneutics," p. 185.

26 Kant, *Critique of Pure Reason*, p. 677.

27 Isaiah Berlin, *The Roots of Romanticism* (ed. Henry Hardy; Princeton: Princeton University Press, 1999), pp. 1–2. Berlin is referring specifically to Romanticism in this quote. He identifies

expressivism (he calls it expressionism) with Romanticism in his section on Herder, see especially p. 58.

28 Brent W. Sockness has made just this case, very convincingly, in an essay titled, "Schleiermacher and the Ethics of Authenticity: The *Monologen* of 1800," *Journal of Religious Ethics* 32/3 (2004), pp. 477–517.

29 Sockness, "Schleiermacher and the Ethics of Authenticity," p. 485.

30 Friedrich Daniel Ernst Schleiermacher, *Monologen. Eine Neujahrsausgabe. Kritische Gesamtausgabe* I.3 (ed. Günter Meckenstock; Berlin: de Gruyter, 1988), pp. 17 and 18. English translation, *Schleiermacher's Soliloquies* (intro. and trans. Horace Leland Friess; Chicago: Open Court, 1926), pp. 30 and 31. Translations from the *Monologen* are mine unless otherwise noted (the second sentence above is Friess's translation).

31 Taylor describes expressivism in the chapter "The Expressivist Turn," in *Sources of the Self: The Making of the Modern Identity* (Cambridge: Harvard University Press, 1989), pp. 368–90; and most fully in the chapter I have cited in Chapter 1 on the challenges facing the Kantian and post-Kantian generation from his book, *Hegel*. For this idea see Taylor, *Hegel*, p. 14.

32 Sockness, "Schleiermacher and the Ethics of Authenticity," p. 486. The Taylor quote is from *Hegel*, p. 16.

33 Goethe, *Wilhelm Meister's Apprenticeship* (ed. and trans. Eric A. Blackall in cooperation with Victor Lange; *Goethe The Collected Works* vol. 9; Princeton: Princeton University Press, 1989), p. 39.

34 Schleiermacher, *Monologen*, p. 32; ET, p. 56.

35 Talal Asad points to this important shift in ideas of agency in chapters 2 ("Thinking about Agency and Pain") and 3 ("Reflections on Cruelty and Torture") of *Formations of the Secular: Christianity, Islam, and Modernity* (Stanford: Stanford University Press, 2003), pp. 67–124.

Chapter Four

1 Mircea Eliade writes that religion involves "the social man, the economic man, and so forth," but that these things do not add up to religion. *See Images and Symbols: Studies in Religious Symbolism* (trans. Philip Mairet; Princeton: Princeton University Press, 1991), p. 32.

2. J. Samuel Preus traces the history of this explanatory approach to religion in *Explaining Religion: Criticism and Theory from Bodin to Freud* (Oxford: Oxford University Press, 1996).
3. Wayne Proudfoot, *Religious Experience* (Berkeley: University of California Press, 1985), p. 31.
4. Russell McCutcheon, *Critics not Caretakers* (Albany: State University of New York Press, 2001), p. 4.
5. Walter Capps, *Religious Studies: The Making of a Discipline* (Minneapolis: Fortress Press, 1995), p. 13.
6. Eric Sharpe, *Comparative Religion: A History* (New York: Charles Scribner's Sons, 1975; reprint, LaSalle: Open Court, 1986), p. 164.
7. Sharpe, *Comparative Religion: A History*, p. 164. I remind readers of our discussion in the Chapter 3, "Hermeneutics," about the way Schleiermacher's use of the term "divination" has been misunderstood.
8. Rudolf Otto, *The Idea of the Holy* (Oxford: Oxford University Press, 1958), p. 8.
9. Francis Schüssler Fiorenza has pointed out the irony in this situation. While the critique of Schleiermacher from the religious studies side has argued that he is too theological to be theoretically useful, much of the critique from the side of theology has been that religion, as defined by Schleiermacher, "fail[s] to take into account the primacy of divine revelation, divine activity, and the specificity of Christian identity." Francis Schüssler Fiorenza, "Religion: A Contested Site in Theology and the Study of Religion," *Harvard Theological Review* 93/1 (2000), p. 13.
10. A further irony is that Otto, who was a careful reader of Schleiermacher, is quite clear about the differences between his theories and Schleiermacher's. In particular Otto objects that Schleiermacher's feeling of absolute dependence, a key term as we will see in Chapter 5, "Mediating Theology," refers to no supernatural object outside the self. Otto, *Idea of the Holy*, p. 10.
11. George Lindbeck, *The Nature of Doctrine: Religion and Theology in a Postliberal Age* (Louisville: Westminster John Knox Press, 1984).
12. Wayne Proudfoot, *Religious Experience* (Berkeley: University of California Press, 1985).
13. Lindbeck, *The Nature of Doctrine*, p. 16.
14. Lindbeck, *The Nature of Doctrine*, p. 21.
15. Lindbeck, *The Nature of Doctrine*, p. 17.

16 Lindbeck's interpretation of Schleiermacher was quickly refuted in a review of *The Nature of Doctrine* by B. A. Gerrish in the *Journal of Religion* 68/1 (1988), pp. 87–92. Gerrish points out that "in Schleiermacher's view, doctrines do not express a prelinguistic experience but an experience that has already been constituted by the language of the community," p. 90.

17 As Gerrish writes, Lindbeck "should count himself among Schleiermacher's friends." Gerrish, review of *The Nature of Doctrine*, p. 92.

18 Proudfoot, *Religious Experience*, p. 31. I have formulated Proudfoot's argument in terms of these three claims in a previous article, "Anschauung and Intuition, Again," in *Schleiermacher, the Study of Religion, and the Future of Theology* (ed. Brent W. Sockness and Wilhelm Gräb; Berlin: de Gruyter, 2010), pp. 42–43.

19 Proudfoot, *Religious Experience*, p. 24.

20 Proudfoot, *Religious Experience*, p. 31.

21 I have been a copanelist with Wayne Proudfoot at two separate Schleiermacher conferences, one at The University of Chicago (2008) and one at the University of Marburg (2010). Our lively conversations (including Andrew Dole, also a member of both these panels) have sharpened my thinking immeasurably. Proudfoot has acknowledged that his earlier reading of Schleiermacher may need to be modified. See "Immediacy and Intentionality in the Feeling of Absolute Dependence," in *Schleiermacher, the Study of Religion, and the Future of Theology* (ed. Brent W. Sockness and Wilhelm Gräb; Berlin: de Gruyter, 2010), pp. 27–37. But Proudfoot still holds that there is something fishy and un-Kantian about Schleiermacher's theory of religion. While agreeing that it is more accurate to see Schleiermacher as arguing that intuitions depend on each person's formation (*Interpreting Religion*, 89), it is still the case that Schleiermacher differentiates religion from Kantian morality and Fichtean philosophy (p. 91) by arguing that religious intuitions are distinctive and unconnected, and thus balance the activity on the universe of morals and metaphysics with religion's passive reception of the universe. Proudfoot's point is that it is hard to see how one can be embedded in causal relations and have intuitions that are independent and unconnected. This is an astute point, too complex to take up adequately here. For further discussion see chapter 1 of my *Modern Religion, Modern Race* (forthcoming).

22 Andrew Dole, "The Case of the Disappearing Discourse: Schleiermacher's Fourth Speech and the Field of Religious Studies," *The Journal of Religion* 88/1 (January 2008), p. 7.

23 Wilhelm Dilthey, "Development of Hermeneutics," in *Wilhelm Dilthey's Selected Writings* (ed. and trans. H. P. Rickman; Cambridge: Cambridge University Press, 1976), pp. 258 and 260. I follow here Dole's discussion on pages 27–31 of *Schleiermacher on Religion and the Natural Order* (New York: Oxford University Press, 2010). Dole has substituted the German *Geisteswissenschaften* for Rickman's translation, "sciences of man."

24 One reliable indicator that a scholar is recycling the standard (old-fashioned, I argue) reading of Schleiermacher on religion is that they cite the John Oman translation of the third edition of the *Speeches* rather than the more recent translation of the first edition by Richard Crouter. See John C. Oman, trans., *On Religion: Speeches to Its Cultured Despisers* (Louisville: Westminster John Knox, 1994); Richard Crouter, trans., *On Religion: Speeches to Its Cultured Despisers* (Cambridge: Cambridge University Press, 1996). A "synoptic" edition of the *Speeches* has just been published that allows readers to compare all three editions. See *Über die Religion. Reden an die Gebildeten unter ihren Verächtern. 1799/1806/1821. Studienausgabe* (ed. Niklaus Peter, Frank Besterbreutje, and Anna Büsching; Zürich: Theologischer Verlag Zürich, 2012). See a review of this edition by Friedrich Wilhelm Graf in the *Neue Zürcher Zeitung* October 9, 2012.

25 Much of the debate about Schleiermacher's theory of religion has in fact been a debate about Eliade's theory of religion. The "History of Religions" approach to comparative religions was brought to The University of Chicago by Joachim Wach in 1956, and became the dominant school of the academic study of religions in the United States under his successor, Mircea Eliade. Aside from his genius, Eliade's influence in part stems from the fact that he and his colleagues trained so many Ph.D.s at just the moment in the United States when public universities began establishing departments of religion following the 1963 *School District of Abington* v. *Schempp* Supreme Court decision. Thus the first generation of nondivinity school university teachers bears the stamp of his method. In many of his works, most particularly his encyclopedic, three-volume *Comparative Religion*, Eliade shows that diverse religions from all parts of the world share a similar morphology, or shape. By the 1980s a new generation of scholars was reacting against this, arguing that Eliade's focus on underlying similarities was in itself a religious, not scientific, point of view, and that it downplayed important historical and cultural differences between traditions.

26 See discussion of Charles Taylor on this context. Chapter 2, pp. 31–32.

27 Friedrich Schleiermacher, *On Religion: Speeches to Its Cultured Despisers* (trans. Richard Crouter; Cambridge: Cambridge University Press, 1988), pp. 22 and 13. Translations of the *Speeches* in this chapter are Crouter's, which I have checked against the original, *Über die Religion: Reden an die Gebildeten unter ihren Verächtern. KGA* I.2. Citations give page numbers to both.
28 Schleiermacher, *On Religion*, p. 221; ET, p. 32.
29 Kant, *Prolegomena*, p. 33. Kant also defines "intuitions" in *The Critique of Pure Reason* as follows: "Appearances are the only objects that can be given to us immediately, and that in them which is immediately related to the object is called intuition," p. 233.
30 Schleiermacher, *On Religion*, p. 215; ET, p. 26.
31 Kant uses the language of objects being "given" to us in intuition. See *The Critique of Pure Reason*, p. 224.
32 Schleiermacher, *On Religion*, p. 214; ET, p. 25.
33 Schleiermacher, *On Religion*, pp. 213–14; ET, pp. 24–25.
34 Schleiermacher, *On Religion*, p. 218; ET, p. 29.
35 Thus Capps is right to title his chapter "Schleiermacher's Shift to the Aesthetic Mode," but only if by aesthetic we mean what Kant means by aesthetic when he titles a section of his first Critique the "Transcendental Aesthetic." For Kant that signals not a theory of art but an analysis of experience. There is a connection of art and religion for Schleiermacher, not because both are mysterious but because both are individual symbolizing activities in our chart from the *Lectures on Ethics* (Chapter 2, p. 43).
36 Schleiermacher, *On Religion*, p. 211; ET, p. 22.
37 Schleiermacher, *On Religion*, p. 243; ET, p. 51.
38 Schleiermacher, *On Religion*, p. 245; ET, p. 53.
39 Schleiermacher, *On Religion*, p. 295; ET, p. 97.
40 Schleiermacher, *Dialektik*, p. 285.
41 An extremely perceptive reader may have noted a discrepancy in the way I have used "intuition" above. On the one hand, when Schleiermacher discusses intuition, it is usually as an everyday facet of all experience. It is part of our basic cognition. But in Chapter 2 I quoted the following passage from the *Dialectic*: "When the organic aspect predominates, we call this perception. When the intellectual aspect predominates, we call this thinking in the narrow sense. When the organic and intellectual aspects are in balance, we call this intuition" (p. 153). Intuition in this sense is a balance

of the organic and intellectual aspects in intuition. It lies between thinking and perception, narrowly defined. Schleiermacher does not say much more about intuition used in this second sense. One way to understand this second sense of intuition is to say that all experience is intuition, but the particularly balanced and therefore perceptive select few have powerful intuitions that become the basic intuitions that shape others and create a religious view of the universe. I will not push this interpretation too far, since I do not have a lot of textual evidence for it. One of Schleiermacher's points in the Speeches is that artists (the very cultured despisers to whom the Speeches are addressed) are themselves "priests" and "prophets," modern virtuosi whose insights make available to others the infinite in the finite. Far from despising religion, Schleiermacher hopes to convince them that they ought to see it (properly understood) as their natural home.

42 Schleiermacher, *On Religion*, p. 213; ET, p. 24.
43 It is helpful to me to think of this as analogous to de Saussure's account of language in *Course in General Linguistics*. Words have meaning not by reference to things, nor by virtue of their etymologies, but because of their synchronic relation to every other word in a language system. See Ferdinand de Saussure, *Course in General Linguistics* (New York: McGraw-Hill Book Company, 1959).
44 Schleiermacher, *On Religion*, p. 227; ET, p. 36.
45 Schleiermacher, *On Religion*, p. 227; ET, p. 36.
46 Schleiermacher, *On Religion*, p. 267; ET, p. 163. Translation is mine.
47 Schleiermacher, *Monologen*, p. 23; ET, p. 31. Translation here is Friess's.
48 Friedrich Schleiermacher, *Die praktische Theologie nach den Grundsätzen der evangelischen Kirche im Zusammenhange dargestellt, Friedrich Schleiermacher's sämmtliche Werke* I.13 (ed. Jacob Frerichs; Berlin: Reimer, 1850), p. 8. Translations from the Practical Theology are mine.
49 Schleiermacher, *On Religion*, 193; ET, p. 82. Translation is Crouter's.
50 Schleiermacher, *On Religion*, pp. 268; ET, p. 164. Translation is mine.
51 Dole, *Schleiermacher on Religion and the Natural Order*, pp. 72–76.
52 Dole, *Schleiermacher on Religion and the Natural Order*, p. 73.

53 Dole, *Schleiermacher on Religion and the Natural Order*, p. 77.
54 Ernst Troeltsch, "What Does the 'Essence of Christianity' Mean?" trans. Michael Pye in *Writings on Theology and Religion* (ed. and trans. Robert Morgan and Michael Pye; Atlanta: Knox, 1977), p. 141, cited by Dole, *Schleiermacher on Religion and the Natural Order*, p. 79. Emphasis in original.
55 Schleiermacher, *Monologen*, p. 46; ET, p. 56. Translation is mine.
56 Schleiermacher, *Praktische Theologie*, p. 68.
57 Dole, *Schleiermacher on Religion and the Natural Order*, p. 107.
58 Schleiermacher, *On Religion*, p. 314; ET, pp. 113–14.
59 Jonathan Z. Smith, *Imagining Religion: From Babylon to Jonestown* (Chicago: University of Chicago Press, 1982), p. xi.
60 Talal Asad points out that definitions of religion that assume a separation of religion and politics, and that make religion into a matter essentially of meaning and belief, serve to exclude certain religions (Islam in particular) from the sphere of legitimate discourse. See among other writings, "The Construction of Religion as an Anthropological Category," in *Genealogies of Religion: Discipline and Reasons of Power in Christianity and Islam* (Baltimore: Johns Hopkins University Press, 1993), pp. 27–54.
61 See p. 43.
62 See here José Casanova, *Public Religions in the Modern World* (Chicago: University of Chicago Press, 1994), esp. chapter 1: "Secularization, Enlightenment, and Modern Religion," pp. 11–39.
63 See Schleiermacher's *Briefe bei Gelegenheit der politisch theologischen Aufgabe des Sendschreibens jüdischer Hausväter* (1799). *Schleiermacher's Letters*, along with the two anonymous letters to which they respond, and the response of Wilhelm Abraham Teller, have been translated by Richard Crouter and Julie Klassen in *A Debate on Jewish Emancipation and Christian Theology in Old Berlin* (Indianapolis: Hackett, 2004). It is important to add that while Schleiermacher advocated for Jewish citizenship, he also believed that Judaism would have to be reformed to come into closer alignment with what I have called ideal external religion above.
64 For a full account of these issues see Theodore Vial, *Modern Religion, Modern Race* (forthcoming).
65 Robert Orsi provides a useful discussion of this issue in the history religious studies, though without specific reference to Schleiermacher, in *Between Heaven and Earth: The Religious*

Worlds People Make and the Scholars Who Study Them (Princeton: Princeton University Press, 2005), esp. chapter 6: "Snakes Alive: Religious Studies between Heaven and Earth." Orsi is free with his normative judgments, but he is also clear that the study of American Catholicism has often been marred by the unthinking application of Protestant-inflected categories.

Chapter Five

1 Gerrish, *A Prince of the Church*, p. 26.
2 Friedrich Schleiermacher, *Der christliche Glaube nach den Grundsätzen der evangelischen Kirche im Zusammenhange dargestellt*. KGA I.13, pp. 1–2 (Rolf Schäfer edn; Berlin: de Gruyter, 2nd edn, 2003), §16.1, pp. 130–31; ET, pp. 78–79. I cite *The Christian Faith* by proposition number, section number, and page.
3 I write this without my usual caveats about the social nature of speech and experience only because we have covered that thoroughly in Chapters 2, 3, and 4. Given those chapters I trust the reader not to misread my statements here as the old-fashioned view of Schleiermacher dubbed by Lindbeck "experiential-expressivism."
4 Schleiermacher, *Der christliche Glaube*, §16.2, p. 132; ET, pp. 78–79.
5 For a groundbreaking analysis of Schleiermacher's use of creeds in *The Christian Faith* see Walter Wyman, "The Role of the Protestant Confessions in Schleiermacher's *The Christian Faith*," *Journal of Religion* 87/3 (July 2007), pp. 355–85.
6 Gerrish, *Prince of the Church*, p. 33; Walter E. Wyman, Jr, "Sin and Redemption," in *The Cambridge Companion to Schleiermacher* (ed. Jacqueline Mariña; Cambridge: Cambridge University Press, 2005), p. 144.
7 David Friedrich Strauss attended and took notes on the 1831–32 lectures.
8 Friedrich Schleiermacher, *Kurze Darstellung des theologischen Studiums*. KGA I.6 (ed. Dirk Schmid; Berlin: de Gruyter, 1998). A good English translation is available: see Terrence N. Tice, trans., *Brief Outline of Theology as a Field of Study* (rev. translation of the 1811 and 1830 edns; Louisville: Westminster John Knox Press, 2011).
9 *Kurze Darstellung* §25, p. 14; ET, p. 25.

10 *Kurze Darstellung* §24, p. 13; ET, p. 25.
11 Theological study is rounded out with what Schleiermacher calls Church Statistics, by which he means the present state of the relevant congregations. In contemporary seminaries sometimes this takes the form of courses in the sociology of religion.
12 A nuanced but intentionally accessible account of Schleiermacher's Christology can be found in Catherine L. Kelsey, *Thinking about Christ with Schleiermacher* (Louisville: Westminster John Knox Press, 2003).
13 Gerrish, *Prince of the Church*, p. 48.
14 Wyman, "Sin and Redemption," p. 143.
15 *The Christian Faith* §4.1, pp. 33–34; ET, p. 13.
16 *The Christian Faith* §4.3, p. 38; ET, p. 16.
17 *The Christian Faith* §4.4, pp. 38–39; ET, p. 16.
18 This particular wording, which I find felicitous, was suggested to me by Walter Wyman in a personal communication, September 2, 2012.
19 Gerrish, *Prince of the Church*, 40.
20 *The Christian Faith* §94.2, pp. 54–55; ET, p. 387.
21 See *The Christian Faith* §97.4.
22 Friedrich Daniel Ernst Schleiermacher, "Über seine Glaubenslehre an Herrn Dr. Lücke, zwei Sendschreiben," *Theologische Studien und Kritiken*, pp. 255–84 and 481–532. The letters appear in KGA I.10 (Berlin: de Gruyter, 1990). A good English translation with excellent introduction is available: *On the Glaubenslehre* (trans. James Duke and Francis Fiorenza; Chico: Scholars Press, 1981). Scholars typically refer to this very important source of information on Schleiermacher's theology as "Letters to Lücke" or "On the *Glaubenslehre*."
23 "Letters to Lücke," p. 339; ET, p. 56.
24 This is the root of the criticisms against him launched by Hegel and his followers. See B. A. Gerrish, "Friedrich Schleiermacher," in *Continuing the Reformation: Essays on Modern Religious Thought* (Chicago: University of Chicago Press, 1993), p. 171.
25 Karl Barth, *The Theology of Schleiermacher* (ed. Dietrich Ritschl; trans. Geoffrey Bromiley; Grand Rapids: Eerdmans, 1982), p. 275.
26 "The feeling that Schleiermacher specifies assumes the concept of absolute dependence and appears also to assume the concept of God." Proudfoot, *Religious Experience*, p. 20.
27 Pages here refer to Schleiermacher, *Vorlesungen über die Dialektik*.

28 Richard R. Niebuhr, *Schleiermacher on Christ and Religion: A New Introduction* (New York: Charles Scribner's Sons, 1964), pp. 161–62, 211–12. Cited in Gerrish, "Friedrich Schleiermacher," p. 176.
29 In the following discussion I follow closely the analysis of Walter E. Wyman, Jr, "Sin and Redemption," in *The Cambridge Companion to Schleiermacher* (ed. Jacqueline Mariña; Cambridge: Cambridge University Press, 2005), pp. 29–149.
30 *The Christian Faith* §66, p. 405; ET, p. 271.
31 Wyman, "Sin and Redemption," p. 133.
32 *The Christian Faith* §72.3, p. 445; Wyman, "Sin and Redemption," p. 134.
33 Wyman, "Sin and Redemption," p. 136.
34 *The Christian Faith* §75.1, p. 472; ET, p. 316.
35 John Calvin, *Institutes of the Christian Religion* (ed. John T. McNeill; trans. Ford Lewis Battles; Philadelphia: Westminster Press, 1960), Book III, chapter II, part 8, p. 551.
36 *The Christian Faith* §101.2, p. 114; ET, p. 432.
37 *The Christian Faith* §101.2, p. 115; ET, p. 433.

Chapter Six

1 Much of the material for this chapter is taken from my chapter, "Schleiermacher and the State," in *The Cambridge Companion to Schleiermacher* (ed. Jacqueline Mariña; Cambridge: Cambridge University Press, 2005), pp. 269–85. The definitive account of Schleiermacher's political thought and activity is Matthias Wolfes's *Öffentlichkeit und Bürgergesellschaft. Friedrich Schleiermachers politische Wirksamkeit* (2 vols; Berlin: Walter de Gruyter, 2004). As I was preparing this chapter Miriam Rose's book *Schleiermachers Staatslehre* appeared (Tübingen: Mohr Siebeck, 2011). She cites favorably my focus on placing Schleiermacher's political thought in the context of his biography and the political events of his day. Her focus is more on placing Schleiermacher in contemporaneous debates about political philosophy.
2 There was, of course, the Holy Roman Empire, that included much of what became Germany. It also included parts of what was later Italy and Burgundy. As Voltaire quipped, it was neither Holy, Roman, nor an empire. It dissolved in 1806 during Napoleon's invasions.

NOTES

3 See Catherine Kelsey, Schleiermacher's *Preaching, Dogmatics, and Biblical Criticism: The Interpretation of Jesus Christ in the Gospel of John* (Eugene: Wipf & Stock, 2007).

4 Cited in James J. Sheehan, *German History, 1770–1866 Oxford History of Modern Europe* (Oxford: Oxford University Press, 1989), p. 379.

5 Dilthey, "Schleiermacher's politische Gesinnung und Wirksamkeit," in *Zur Preussischen Geschichte* vol. 12 *Wilhelm Dilthey Gesammelte Schriften* (Stuttgart: B. G. Teubner, 1960), pp. 1–2.

6 Karl Freiherr vom und zum Stein, "Über die zweckmässige Bildung der obersten und der Provinzial, Finanz und Polizey Behörden in der Preussischen Monarchie," the so-called Nassauer Denkschrift, in Stein, *Briefwechsel, Denkschriften und Aufzeichnungen* (n.p., 1931), vol. II, p. 227.

7 Friedrich Schleiermacher, "Vorlesungen über Politik gehalten von Schleiermacher im Sommer 1829: Nachschriften von Hess und Willich," in *KGA* II.8, pp. 499–500. I cite this manuscript as *Die Lehre vom Staat* (HeWi), following the abbreviations of the *KGA*'s editor. This is the fullest set of notes from Schleiermacher's lectures on the state. Schleiermacher's own notes that were the basis of this semester's lectures I cite as Schleiermacher, *Die Lehre vom Staat* (1829).

8 Schleiermacher, *Die Lehre vom Staat* (1829), p. 69.

9 Schleiermacher, *Die Lehre vom Staat* (HeWi), pp. 507–08.

10 Schleiermacher, *Die Lehre vom Staat* (HeWi), pp. 511, 512.

11 Schleiermacher, *Die Lehre vom Staat* (HeWi), p. 509.

12 Schleiermacher, *On Religion, KGA* I.2, p. 268; ET, pp. 73–74.

13 Schleiermacher, *The Christian Faith*, § 6.2; ET, p. 27.

14 Schleiermacher, *Monologen, KGA* I.3, p. 32.

15 Dilthey, "Schleiermacher's politische Gesinnung und Wirksamkeit," pp. 12–13.

16 Schleiermacher, *Predigten, SW* II.1, pp. 246–61. These sermons are not yet available in the *KGA*, so I cite from the older *Sämmtliche Werke*. Schleiermacher preached this sermon on March 28, 1813. On March 17 the King had ended a long period of wavering and issued a call for troops to join the Russians in attacking Napoleon.

17 Schleiermacher, *SW* II.1, pp. 251–52.

18 I translate Ephesians from Schleiermacher's German text.

19 *SW* II.1, pp. 218–32.

20 *SW* II.1, pp. 356–69.

21 Benedict Anderson has pointed to the role of newspapers in creating modern national identities, in part by relying on and bringing into existence "imagined communities" of readers who are geographically distant from one another and do not know one another personally but who have common interests and perceive themselves to be part of the same group. See *Imagined Communities: Reflections on the Origin and Spread of Nationalism* (New York: Verso, rev. and extended edn, 1991).

22 Matthias Wolfes identifies three important themes of Schleiermacher' editorship, only the first of which I discuss here. See Wolfes, *Öffentlichkeit und Bürgergesellschaft*, vol. 1, pp. 436–42.

23 *KGA* I.9, p. 64.

24 *KGA* I.9, p. 218 n. 8.

25 Nowak, *Schleiermacher*, p. 387.

26 *KGA* I.9, p. 395.

27 *KGA* I.9, p. 471.

SELECT BIBLIOGRAPHY

Works by Schleiermacher

German

Beginning in 1984 a critical edition (*Kritische Gesamtausgabe*) of Schleiermacher's works has begun to be published. Forty volumes are planned in five divisions. The volumes of this critical edition are uniformly of excellent quality, and have fueled much of the renaissance in Schleiermacher scholarship since their appearance. I follow the standard citation practice for the critical edition by abbreviating it as *KGA*, followed by division number, and volume (additional numbers indicate multivolume works), followed by page number in the footnotes. For example, the lectures on Dialectic are in the second division, volume 10, and take up two volumes: *KGA* II.10, 1–2.

For writings not yet published in the critical edition I have normally relied on an earlier collected works, *Schleiermachers sämmtliche Werke*, published in the 1860s. These editions are cited as *SW*, followed by division number and volume (so, Schleiermacher's *Practical Theology* is division I, volume 13: I.13.) The texts in this edition are often conglomerations of manuscripts put together by the editor to form a more complete text. While useful, it is not a critical edition and lacks the scholarly apparatus that allows a scholar to see the development in Schleiermacher's thought as he lectured on the same topic over time, or revised works for second and third editions of his publications.

Schleiermacher, Friedrich Daniel Ernst, *Vorlesungen über die Kirchengeschichte. KGA* II.6 (ed. Simon Gerber; Berlin: de Gruyter, 2006).
— "Aufzeichnung zum Kolleg 1811," *KGA* II.10, 1 *Vorlesungen über die Dialektik* (ed. Andreas Arndt; Berlin: Walter de Gruyter, 2002).
— *Aus Schleiermacher's Leben. In Briefen* (Band 2; Berlin: G. Reimer, 1861).

— *Der christliche Glaube nach den Grundsätzen der evangelischen Kirche im Zusammenhange dargestellt.* KGA I.13, 1–2 (ed. Rolf Schäfer; Berlin: de Gruyter, 2nd edn, 2003).

— "Gespräch zweier selbst überlegender evangelischer Christen über die Schrift: Luther in Bezug auf die neue preussische Agende. Ein letztes Wort oder ein erstes" ["Conversation of Two Self-Reflective Evangelical Christians on the Book: Luther in Relation to the New Prussian Church Service. A Final Word or a First One"]. KGA I.9 (ed. Günter Meckenstock with Hans-Friedrich Traulsen; Berlin: de Gruyter, 2000).

— *Hermeneutik und Kritik* (ed. with an introduction by Manfred Frank; Frankfurt am Main: Suhrkamp, 1977).

— *Kirchenpolitische Schriften.* KGA I.9 (ed. Günter Meckenstock with Hans-Friedrich Traulsen; Berlin: de Gruyter, 2000).

— *Kurze Darstellung des theologischen Studiums.* KGA I.6 (ed. Dirk Schmid; Berlin: de Gruyter, 1998).

— *Monologen. Eine Neujahrsausgabe.* KGA I.3 (ed. Günter Meckenstock; Berlin: de Gruyter, 1988).

— *Die praktische Theologie nach den Grundsätzen der evangelischen Kirche im Zusammenhange dargestellt. Friedrich Schleiermacher's sämmtliche Werke* I.13 (ed. Jacob Frerichs; Berlin: Reimer, 1850).

— *Predigten. Friedrich Schleiermacher's sämmtliche Werke* II.1.

— *Über die Religion: Reden an die Gebildeten unter ihren Verächtern (1799), Schriften aus der Berliner Zeit 1796–1799.* KGA I.2 (ed. Günter Meckenstock; Berlin: de Gruyter, 1984).

— *Über die Religion. Reden an die Gebildeten unter ihren Verächtern. 1799/1806/1821. Studienausgabe* (ed. Niklaus Peter, Frank Besterbreutje, and Anna Büsching; Zürich: Theologischer Verlag Zürich, 2012).

— "Über seine Glaubenslehre an Herrn Dr. Lücke, zwei Sendschreiben," *Theologische-dogmatische Abhandlungen und Gelegenheitsschriften.* KGA I.10 (ed. Hans-Friedrich Traulsen with Martin Ohst; Berlin: de Gruyter, 1990).

— *Vorlesungen über die Dialektik.* KGA II.10, 1–2 (ed. Andreas Arndt; Berlin: de Gruyter, 2002).

— *Vorlesungen über die Lehre vom Staat.* KGA II.8 (ed. Walter Jaeschke; Berlin: de Gruyter, 1998).

English Translations

Schleiermacher, Friedrich Daniel Ernst, *Brief Outline of Theology as a Field of Study* (rev. translation of the 1811 and 1830 edns; trans. Terrence N. Tice; Louisville: Westminster John Knox Press, 2011).

— *Briefe bei Gelegenheit der politisch theologischen Aufgabe des Sendschreibens jüdischer Hausväter* (1799) in *A Debate on Jewish Emancipation and Christian Theology in Old Berlin* (trans. Richard Crouter and Julie Klassen; Indianapolis: Hackett, 2004).
— *The Christian Faith* (ed. H. R. MacKintosh and J. S. Stewart; Edinburgh: T&T Clark, 2nd edn, 1986).
— *Dialectic or, The Art of Doing Philosophy: A Study Edition of the 1811 Notes* (trans. Terrence N. Tice; Oxford: Oxford University Press, 2000).
— *Hermeneutics and Criticism and Other Writings* (trans. and ed. Andrew Bowie; Cambridge: Cambridge University Press, 1998).
— *Lectures on Philosophical Ethics* (Cambridge Texts in the History of Philosophy; ed. Robert B. Louden; trans. Louise Adey Huish; Cambridge: Cambridge University Press, 2002).
— *On Religion: Speeches to Its Cultured Despisers* (Cambridge Texts in the History of Philosophy; ed. and trans. Richard Crouter; Cambridge: Cambridge University Press, 1st edn, 1988).
— *On Religion: Speeches to Its Cultured Despisers* (trans. John C. Oman; Louisville: Westminster John Knox, 3rd edn, 1994).
— *On the Glaubenslehre* (trans. James Duke and Francis Fiorenza; Chico: Scholars Press, 1981).
— "The Power of Prayer in Relation to Outward Circumstances," in a republished collection titled *Selected Sermons of Friedrich Schleiermacher* (trans. Mary Wilson; Eugene: Wipf & Stock, n.d.)
— *Schleiermacher's Soliloquies* (Intro. and trans. Horace Leland Friess; Chicago: Open Court, 1926).
— *Servant of the Word: Selected Sermons of Friedrich Schleiermacher* (ed. and trans. Dawn DeVries; Philadelphia: Fortress Press, 1987).

Other Primary Sources

Calvin, John, *Institutes of the Christian Religion* (ed. John T. McNeill; trans. Ford Lewis Battles; Philadelphia: Westminster Press, 1960).
Goethe, Johann Wolfgang von, *Wilhelm Meister's Apprenticeship* (ed. and trans. Eric A. Blackall in cooperation with Victor Lange; *Goethe The Collected Works*; Vol. 9; Princeton: Princeton University Press, 1989).
Hume, David, *An Enquiry Concerning Human Understanding* and *A Letter from a Gentleman to His Friend in Edinburgh* (ed. Eric Steinberg; Indianapolis: Hackett, 1977).
Kant, Immanuel, *Critique of Pure Reason* (Cambridge Edition of the Works of Immanuel Kant; ed. and trans. Paul Guyer and Allen W. Wood; Cambridge: Cambridge University Press, 1998).

— *Foundations of the Metaphysics of Morals and What Is Enlightenment?* (Library of Liberal Arts; trans. Lewis White Beck; Upper Saddle River, NJ: Prentice Hall, 1995).
— "On the Use of Teleological Principles in Philosophy (1788)," in *Race* (trans. John Mark Mikkelsen; ed. Robert Bernasconi; Oxford: Blackwell, 2001), pp. 37–56.
— *Prolegomena to Any Future Metaphysics with Selections from the Critique of Pure Reason* (Cambridge Texts in the History of Philosophy; ed. and trans. Gary Hatfield; Cambridge: Cambridge University Press, rev. edn, 2004).
Stein, Karl Freiherr vom und zum, "Über die zweckmässige Bildung der obersten und der Provinzial, Finanz und Polizey Behörden in der Preussischen Monarchie" ("Nassauer Denkschrift") in Stein, *Briefwechsel, Denkschriften und Aufzeichnungen* (1931), n.p.

Secondary Sources

Anderson Benedict, *Imagined Communities: Reflections on the Origin and Spread of Nationalism* (New York: Verso, rev. and extended edn, 1991).
Arndt, Andreas, "Editorische Bericht." Friedrich Daniel Ernst Schleiermacher, *Vorlesungen über die Dialektik. Kritische Gesamtausgabe* [KGA] 10, 1–2 (Berlin: de Gruyter, 2002).
Asad, Talal, *Formations of the Secular: Christianity, Islam, and Modernity* (Stanford: Stanford University Press, 2003).
— *Genealogies of Religion: Discipline and Reasons of Power in Christianity and Islam* (Baltimore: Johns Hopkins University Press, 1993).
Barth, Karl, *The Theology of Schleiermacher* (ed. Dietrich Ritschl; trans. Geoffrey Bromiley; Grand Rapids: Eerdmans, 1982).
Berlin, Isaiah, *The Roots of Romanticism* (ed. Henry Hardy; Princeton: Princeton University Press, 1999).
Blackwell, Albert with Edwina Lawler, *Friedrich Schleiermacher and the Founding of the University of Berlin: The Study of Religion As a Scientific Discipline* (Lewiston: Edwin Mellen Press, 1991).
Brandt, James M., *All Things New: Reform of Church and Society in Schleiermacher's Christian Ethics* (Columbia Series in Reformed Theology; Louisville: Westminster John Knox Press, 2001).
Capps, Walter, *Religious Studies: The Making of a Discipline* (Minneapolis: Fortress Press, 1995).
Casanova, José, *Public Religions in the Modern World* (Chicago: University of Chicago Press, 1994).

Crouter, Richard, *Friedrich Schleiermacher: Between Enlightenment and Romanticism* (Cambridge: Cambridge University Press, 2008).
de Saussure, Ferdinand, *Course in General Linguistics* (New York: McGraw-Hill Book Company, 1959).
Dilthey, Wilhelm, "Development of Hermeneutics," in *Wilhelm Dilthey's Selected Writings* (ed. and trans. H. P. Rickman; Cambridge: Cambridge University Press, 1976).
— *Leben Schleiermachers* (Berlin: G. Reimer, 1870).
— "Schleiermacher's politische Gesinnung und Wirksamkeit." *Zur Preussischen Geschichte*. Vol. 12. *Wilhelm Dilthey Gesammelte Schriften* (Stuttgart: B. G. Teubner, 1960).
Dole, Andrew, "The Case of the Disappearing Discourse: Schleiermacher's Fourth Speech and the Field of Religious Studies," *Journal of Religion* 88/1 (January 2008).
— *Schleiermacher on Religion and the Natural Order* (New York: Oxford University Press, 2010).
Eliade, Mircea, *Images and Symbols: Studies in Religious Symbolism* (trans. Philip Mairet; Princeton: Princeton University Press, 1991).
Forster, Michael N., "Herder's Philosophy of Language, Interpretation, and Translation: Three Fundamental Principles," *Review of Metaphysics* 56 (December 2002).
Forstman, Jack, *A Romantic Triangle: Schleiermacher and Early German Romanticism* (Missoula: Scholars Press, 1977).
— "The Understanding of Language by Friedrich Schlegel and Schleiermacher," *Soundings* 51 (1968), 146–65.
Francis Schüssler Fiorenza, "Religion: A Contested Site in Theology and the Study of Religion," *Harvard Theological Review* 93/1 (2000).
Gadamer, Hans-Georg, "The Problem of Language in Schleiermacher's Hermeneutics," in *Schleiermacher as Contemporary* (ed. Robert Funk; New York: Herder and Herder, 1970).
— *Truth and Method* (ed. Joel C. Weinsheimer and Donald G. Marshall; London: Continuum, 2nd rev. edn, 1993).
Gerrish, B. A., "Friedrich Schleiermacher," in *Continuing the Reformation: Essays on Modern Religious Thought* (Chicago: University of Chicago Press, 1993).
— *A Prince of the Church: Schleiermacher and the Beginnings of Modern Theology* (Philadelphia: Fortress Press, 1984).
— Review of George Lindbeck, *The Nature of Doctrine. Journal of Religion* 68/1 (1988), pp. 87–92.
Graf, Friedrich Wilhelm, "Ursprüngliches Gefühl unmittelbarer Koinzidenz des Differenten: Zur Modifikation des Religionsbegriff in den verschiedenen Auflagen von Schleiermachers 'Reden über die Religion,'" *Zeitschrift für Theologie und Kirche* 75 (1978), 147–86.

— Review of Peter Studienausgabe edition of *Über die Religion*. *Neue Zürcher Zeitung* October 9, 2012.
Guyer, Paul and Allen Wood, "Introduction to the *Critique of Pure Reason*" (The Cambridge Edition of the Works of Immanuel Kant; Cambridge: Cambridge University Press, 1998).
Holbern, Hajo, *A History of Modern Germany 1648–1840* (New York: Alfred A. Knopf, 1961).
Hübener, Wolfgang, "Schleiermacher und die hermeneutische Tradition," in *Internationaler Schleiermacher-Kongress* (ed. Ebeling Birkner and Selge Kimmerle; Berlin: de Gruyter, 1985), pp. 561–74.
Kelsey, Catherine L., *Schleiermacher's Preaching, Dogmatics, and Biblical Criticism: The Interpretation of Jesus Christ in the Gospel of John* (Eugene: Wipf & Stock, 2007).
— *Thinking about Christ with Schleiermacher* (Louisville: Westminster John Knox Press, 2003).
Kimmerle, Heinz, "Forward to the German Edition," and "Editor's Introduction," in *Hermeneutics: The Handwritten Manuscripts* (F. D. E. Schleiermacher; ed. Kimmerle; trans. James Duke and Jack Forstman; Atlanta: Scholars Press, 1977).
Lamm, Julia A., *The Living God: Schleiermacher's Theological Appropriation of Spinoza* (University Park: Pennsylvania State University Press, 1996).
Lindbeck, George, *The Nature of Doctrine: Religion and Theology in a Postliberal Age* (Louisville: Westminster John Knox Press, 1984).
Lonergan, Bernard, *Insight: A Study of Human Understanding* (Toronto: University of Toronto Press, 5th edn, 1992).
Mariña, Jacqueline, *Transformation of the Self in the Thought of Friedrich Schleiermacher* (Oxford: Oxford University Press, 2008).
Marshall, Bruce D., "Hermeneutics and Dogmatics in Schleiermacher's Theology," *The Journal of Religion* 67/1 (January 1987).
McCutcheon, Russell, *Critics not Caretakers* (Albany: State University of New York Press, 2001).
Nicol, Iain G., *Friedrich Schleiermacher on Creeds, Confessions and Church Union: That They May Be One* (Lewiston: Edwin Mellen, 2004).
Niebuhr, Richard R., *Schleiermacher on Christ and Religion: A New Introduction* (New York: Charles Scribner's Sons, 1964).
Nowak, Kurt, *Schleiermacher: Leben, Werk und Wirkung* (Göttingen: Vandenhoeck & Ruprecht, 2001).
Orsi, Robert, *Between Heaven and Earth: The Religious Worlds People Make and the Scholars Who Study Them* (Princeton: Princeton University Press, 2005).

Otto, Rudolf, *The Idea of the Holy* (Oxford: Oxford University Press, 1958).
Palmer, Richard E., *Hermeneutics: Interpretation Theory in Schleiermacher, Dilthey, Heidegger, and Gadamer* (Evanston: Northwestern University Press, 1969).
Pearson, Lori, *Beyond Essence: Ernst Troeltsch as Historian and Theorist of Christianity* (Harvard Theological Studies 58; Harvard Divinity School; Cambridge: Harvard University Press, 2008).
Preus, J. Samuel, *Explaining Religion: Criticism and Theory from Bodin to Freud* (Oxford: Oxford University Press, 1996).
Proudfoot, Wayne, "Immediacy and Intentionality in the Feeling of Absolute Dependence," in *Schleiermacher, the Study of Religion, and the Future of Theology* (ed. Brent W. Sockness and Wilhelm Gräb; Berlin: de Gruyter, 2010), pp. 27–37.
— *Religious Experience* (Berkeley: University of California Press, 1985).
Raack, R. C., "A New Schleiermacher Letter on the Conspiracy of 1808," *Zeitschrift für Religions- und Geistesgeschichte* 16 (1964), pp. 209–23.
Redeker, Martin, *Friedrich Schleiermacher: Leben und Werk* (Berlin: deGruyter, 1968). English: *Schleiermacher: Life and Thought* (trans. John Wallhausser; Philadelphia: Fortress Press, 1973).
Ricoeur, Paul, "Schleiermacher's Hermeneutics," *Monist* 60/2 (April 1977), pp. 181–97.
Rose, Miriam, *Schleiermachers Staatslehre* (Tübingen: Mohr Siebeck, 2011).
Sharpe, Eric, *Comparative Religion: A History* (New York: Charles Scribner's Sons, 1975; reprint, LaSalle: Open Court, 1986).
Sheehan, James J., *German History, 1770–1866* (Oxford History of Modern Europe; Oxford: Oxford University Press, 1989).
Smith, Jonathan Z., *Imagining Religion: From Babylon to Jonestown* (Chicago: University of Chicago Press, 1982).
Sockness, Brent W., "The Forgotten Moralist: Friedrich Schleiermacher and the Science of Spirit," *Harvard Theological Review* 96/3 (July 2003), pp. 317–48.
— "Schleiermacher and the Ethics of Authenticity: The *Monologen* of 1800," *Journal of Religious Ethics* 32/3 (2004), pp. 477–517.
Taylor, Charles, *Hegel* (Cambridge: Cambridge University Press, 1975).
— *Sources of the Self: The Making of the Modern Identity* (Cambridge: Harvard University Press, 1989).
Tice, Terrence N., *Schleiermacher* (Abingdon Pillars of Theology; Nashville: Abingdon Press, 2006).

Troeltsch, Ernst, "What Does the 'Essence of Christianity' Mean?" Trans. Michael Pye in *Writings on Theology and Religion* (ed. and trans. Robert Morgan and Michael Pye; Atlanta: Knox, 1977).

Vial, Theodore, "Anschauung and Intuition, Again," in *Schleiermacher, the Study of Religion, and the Future of Theology* (ed. Brent W. Sockness and Wilhelm Gräb; Berlin: de Gruyter, 2010).

— "Friedrich Schleiermacher on the Central Place of Worship in Theology," *Harvard Theological Review* 91/1 (1998), pp. 59–73.

— "Schleiermacher and the State," in *The Cambridge Companion to Schleiermacher* (ed. Jacqueline Mariña; Cambridge: Cambridge University Press, 2005), pp. 269–85.

Virmond, Wolfgang, "Neue Textgrundlagungen zu Schleiermacher's früher Hermeneutik: Prolegomena zur kritischen Edition," in *Internationaler Schleiermacher-Kongress* (ed. Ebeling Birkner and Selge Kimmerle; Berlin: de Gruyter, 1985), pp. 575–90.

West, Cornel, "Schleiermacher's Hermeneutics and the Myth of the Given," *Union Seminary Quarterly Review* 34 (1979), pp. 71–84.

Wolfes, Matthias, *Öffentlichkeit und Bürgergesellschaft. Friedrich Schleiermachers politische Wirksamkeit* (2 vols; Berlin: Walter de Gruyter, 2004).

Wyman, Jr, Walter E., "The Role of the Protestant Confessions in Schleiermacher's *The Christian Faith*," *Journal of Religion* 87/3 (July 2007), pp. 355–85.

— "Sin and Redemption," in *The Cambridge Companion to Schleiermacher* (ed. Jacqueline Mariña; Cambridge: Cambridge University Press, 2005), pp. 29–149.

INDEX

absolute dependence 91–2, 95
Anselm 84
Aristotle 35, 56

Barth, Karl 94–5, 99
Berlin, Isaiah 48, 55, 77, 118

Calvin, John 98–9
Capps, Walter 62
cognitive science of religion 78
Council of Chalcedon 93

Dilthey, Wilhelm 4, 65–6, 67, 105, 110
divination 51–2, 62
Dole, Andrew 65, 74–7, 78, 80

Eberhard, Johann August 9
Eliade, Mircea 62, 63, 64, 66, 67
epistemology, Schleiermacher on 33–41

feeling 68, 69–72
Fichte, Johann Gottlieb 12, 13, 21
Frank, Manfred 51, 52
free sociability 43, 76, 80–1
French Revolution 103
Friedrich II (The Great, ruled 1740–1786) 5, 103, 112–13
Friedrich Wilhelm III (ruled 1770–1840) 16, 19, 22, 103, 106, 114–17

Gadamer, Hans-Georg 47, 50, 53–4
genealogy of religion 79–81
Gerrish, B. A. 8, 83, 86, 89–90, 93
Goethe, Johann Wolfgang von 7, 11, 12, 14, 16, 19, 57
Grunow, Eleanore 14, 15

Halle, University of 7, 9, 16–17, 18, 104
Hegel, Georg Wilhelm Friedrich 31, 56, 65–6
Herder, Johann Gottfried 56
Herz, Henriette 11, 12, 13, 15
Humboldt, Wilhelm 12, 19, 56
Hume, David 25
 and cause 26–7, 30

infinite 68, 70, 71–4, 83, 95
intuition 96, 109
Jesus' 92
Kant on 27, 30, 68
Schleiermacher on 67–71, 73

James, William 64
Jesus 8, 88–91, 92–3, 97, 109
Judaism 76, 80

Kant, Immanuel 4, 5, 7, 9, 10, 11, 25, 51, 54–5, 58, 72–3
 dialectic 35
 epistemology 25–30
 metaphysics 29
 moral theory 25, 30–1

Lessing, Gotthold Ephraim 10, 11
Levin, Rahel (later
 Varnhagen) 11, 13
Lindbeck, George 63–4, 68, 70
Lonergan, Bernard 63
Luther, Martin 23, 110, 117

McCutcheon, Russell 62
Marheineke, Philip 22, 116
Marshall, Bruce 51–2
metaphysics, Schleiermacher
 on 35–41
Moravians 5, 6, 7–8, 83, 93

Niebuhr, Richard R. 97
Nowak, Kurt 117

Otto, Rudolf 62, 63, 64, 71

Palmer, Richard E. 50, 51
pantheism 10, 13, 60
Pantheism Controversy 10
Patsch, Hermann 52
piety 68, 75, 92, 94
Proudfoot, Wayne 62, 63, 64–7, 68, 95

reductionism 61–3
Ricoeur, Paul 54

Sack Friedrich Samuel Gottfried 9, 10, 11, 13, 14
Schlegel, Friedrich 12, 13, 14, 15, 104
Schleiermacher, Anne Maria Louise (half-sister, "Nanny," later Arndt) 6
Schleiermacher, Charlotte (sister) 6, 12
Schleiermacher, Henriette (wife; née Mühlenfels) 17, 20
Schleiermacher, Johann Carl (brother) 6
Schleiermacher, Nathaniel (son) 20
Schleyermacher, Daniel (grandfather) 5
Schleyermacher, Elisabeth Maria Katharina (mother; née Stubenrauch) 5
Schleyermacher, Gottlieb (father) 5, 7, 11, 83
science and religion 72
Sharpe, Eric 62
Smith, Jonathan Z. 78–9
Sockness, Brent 56
Spinoza, Baruch 10–11, 13–14
Stein, Karl Freiherr vom 105, 106, 112
Strauss, David Friedrich 99–100
Stubenrauch, Samuel Ernst Timotheus (uncle) 5, 9

Taylor, Charles 25, 48
 expressivism 55–9
 generation following
  Kant 31–2, 45–6, 58–9
Tillich, Paul 63
Troeltsch, Ernst 74

Veit, Dorothea 12–13, 14
Virmond, Wolfgang 52

West, Cornel 51
Willich, Ehrenfried von 16–17, 20
Wolff, Christian 5, 9
Wyman, Walter 86, 90, 97, 100

www.ingramcontent.com/pod-product-compliance
Lightning Source LLC
Chambersburg PA
CBHW060955230426
43665CB00015B/2218